Shaker Architecture

A Shaker Carpenter

Shaker Architecture

Descriptions with Photographs and Drawings
of
Shaker Buildings

At
Mount Lebanon, New York
Watervliet, New York
West Pittsfield, Massachusetts

WILLIAM LAWRENCE LASSITER

Senior Curator of History and Art,
New York State Education Dept.

Illustrated by Constantine Kermes

BONANZA BOOKS · NEW YORK

TO

AMALIA MONTEMAYOR LASSITER

AND

MY SON

WILLIAM LAWRENCE LASSITER

FOREWORD

The Shakers were a religious group. But first of all, they were practical people. The movement had started in Manchester, England. Workers living in the slum areas of this factory town in the 1700's knew economic and moral conditions at their worst. No wonder they sought escape from the bonds and the ugliness of their physical daily lives. No wonder they sought escape to spiritual freedom and beauty. They found the latter first, under the leadership and inspiration of Ann Lee—"Mother Ann." It was not until she led them —a little band of eight followers—across the Atlantic to the port of New York that they also found economic freedom. It was like the admonition in the Bible; "Seek ye first the kingdom of God; and all these things shall be added unto you." But it was a long hard road from their first American home on a tract of wilderness land called Niskayuna (near Albany) before Shaker settlements in this county—the farmlands, the barns, the houses and the churches—became almost a pattern of perfection for the countryside about them.

The Shaker organization was comparatively simple. The Shakers were celibates, owning all things in common. Men and women were equal in power and responsibility. The little band of nine, grown to about six thousand by the middle 1800's, now occupied eighteen prosperous settlements scattered throughout New England, New York, Kentucky, and Ohio. Each separate community was governed by a Ministry consisting of two men and two women (elders and eldresses) who decided all matters of policy. These separate groups of leaders were answerable only to the central ministry at New Lebanon, New York. Thus it was possible to achieve uniformity throughout Shakerdom.

This accounts partly for the similarity of design and workmanship found in Shaker buildings and in furniture. But the absolute integrity of everything the Shakers made stems from three axioms left them by Mother Ann. First of all, she said to them: "Hands to work, and hearts to God." Then she laid down a principle which modern functionalists follow: "Every force evolves a form." And finally this advice: "Do all your work as though you had a thousand years to live, and as you would if you knew you must die tomorrow."

Marguerite Fellows Melcher

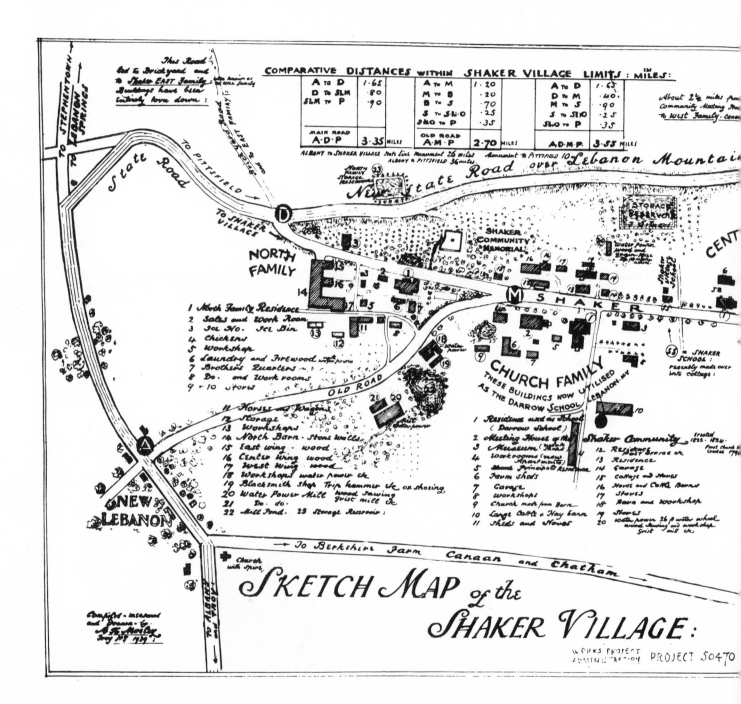

COMPARATIVE DISTANCES WITHIN SHAKER VILLAGE LIMITS: IN MILES:

A to D	1·65		A to M	1·20		A to D	1·65
D to SLM	·80		M to B	·20		D to M	·40
SLM to P	·90		B to S	·70		M to S	·90
			S to SLO	·25		S to SLO	·25
			SLO to P	·35		SLO to P	·35
MAIN ROAD			**OLD ROAD**				
A·D·P	**3·35** MILES		A·M·P	**2·70** MILES		A·D·M·P·	**3·55** MILES

ALBANY to SHAKER VILLAGE State Line Monument 26 miles Monument to Pittsfield 10
ALBANY to PITTSFIELD 36 miles

This Road led to Brickyard and to Shaker EAST Family Buildings have been entirely torn down:

About 2½ miles from Community Meeting House to WEST Family: Cana...

TO STEPHENTOWN
TO LEBANON SPRINGS
State Road
TO PITTSFIELD
TO SHAKER VILLAGE
To SHAKER EAST FAMILY

New State Road over Lebanon Mountain

NORTH FAMILY STORAGE RESERVOIR
STORAGE RESERVOIR
SHAKER COMMUNITY MEMORIAL
WATER POWER WOOD AND GRIST MILL
SHAKER VILLAGE SCHOOL
CENT...

NORTH FAMILY

1 North Family Residence
2 Sales and Work Room
3 Ice Ho. Ice Bin
4 Chickens
5 Workshop
6 Laundry and Firewood with room
7 Brothers Quarters
8 Do. and Work rooms
9 ~ 10 Stores
11 Horse and Wagon
12 Storage
13 Workshops
14 North Barn. Stone walls.
15 East wing ~ wood
16 Center wing ~ wood
17 West wing ~ wood
18 Workshops water power &c
19 Blacksmith shop Trip hammer &c or shoeing
20 Water Power Mill wood sawing grist mill &c
21 Do. do.
22 Mill Pond. 23 Storage Reservoir:

OLD ROAD

WATER POWER
MILL WATER POWER

SHAKER

M

CHURCH FAMILY
THESE BUILDINGS NOW UTILISED AS THE DARROW SCHOOL

1 Residence used as School (Darrow School)
2 Meeting House of the Shaker Community
3 Museum (Church Home)
4 Work rooms (now apartments)
5 Stand Principal Residence
6 Farm sheds
7 Garage
8 Workshops
9 Church made from Barn
10 Large Cattle & Hay barn
11 Sheds and Stoves

12 Residence West Office &c
13 Residence
14 Garage
15 Cottage and Stores
16 Horse and Cattle Barns
17 Stores
18 Barn and workshop
19 Stores
20 Water power 26 ft water wheel wood sawing and work shop grist mill &c

erected 1822. 1824.
First Church erected 1790.

SS = SHAKER SCHOOL: presently made over into cottages.

▲ NEW LEBANON

TO BERKSHIRE FARM CANAAN and CHATHAM

FROM ALBANY

✝ Church with spire

Compiled · measured and Drawn by
A. F. Morley
July N.Y. 1939:

SKETCH MAP of the
SHAKER VILLAGE:

WORKS PROJECT ADMINISTRATION PROJECT 50470

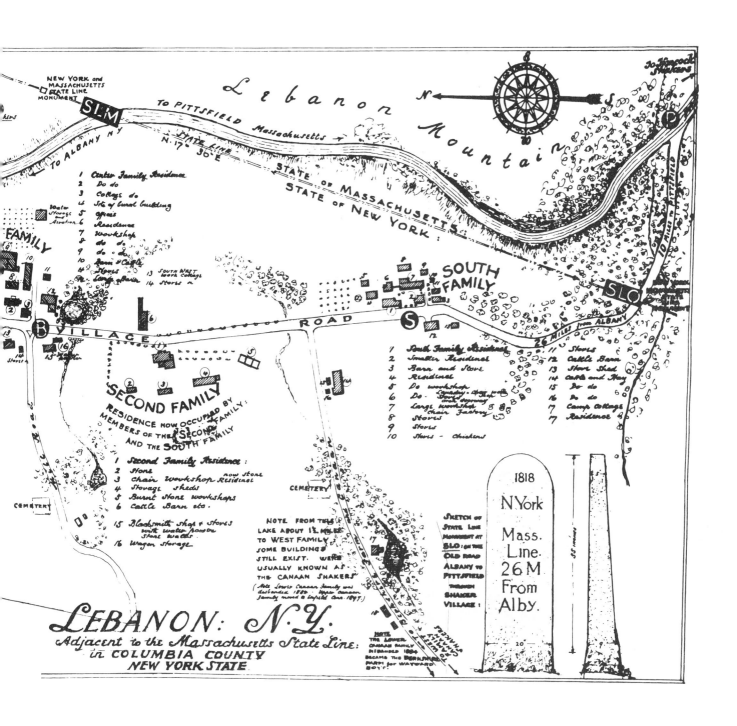

LEBANON: N.Y.
Adjacent to the Massachusetts State Line
in COLUMBIA COUNTY
NEW YORK STATE

CONTENTS

FOREWORD

By Margaret Fellows Melcher

INTRODUCTION
Page 13

STONE BARN — NORTH FAMILY
Page 25

DWELLING HOUSE — NORTH FAMILY
Page 32

LAUNDRY BUILDING — NORTH FAMILY
Page 45

LUMBER AND GRIST MILL — NORTH FAMILY
Page 52

BRETHREN'S RED BRICK SHOP — NORTH FAMILY
Page 58

MEETING HOUSE — CHURCH FAMILY
Page 65

MINISTRY'S DWELLING HOUSE — CHURCH FAMILY
Page 81

BLACKSMITH'S SHOP — CHURCH FAMILY
Page 88

SHAKER SCHOOL — CHURCH FAMILY
Page 93

SISTERS' WORKSHOP — SOUTH FAMILY
Page 99

MAIN DWELLING HOUSE — WEST FAMILY
Page 109

"ROUND BARN" HANCOCK SHAKERS
Page 123

A SUGGESTED BIBLIOGRAPHY
Page 127

LIST OF ILLUSTRATIONS

Frontispiece — *Shaker Carpenter*

The Stone Barn — Page 24

Stone Barn — Page 25

Dwelling House — Page 32

Sisters' Room — Page 33

Laundry Building — Page 45

Sister Folding Towels — Page 51

Lumber and Grist Mill — Page 52

A Shaker Carpenter — Page 57

Brethren's Red Brick Shop — Page 58

In the Shoemaker's Shop — Page 60

Meeting House — Page 65

An entrance to the Meeting House — Page 80

Ministry's Dwelling House — Page 81

Members of the Ministry — Page 83

Blacksmith's Shop — Page 88

In the Blacksmith's Shop — Page 89

Shaker School — Page 93

The Schoolmaster and His Pupils — Page 94

Sisters' Workshop — Page 99

In the Sisters' Sewing Room — Page 108

Main Dwelling House — Page 109

Off-Center Double Doors — Page 111

Round Barn — Page 123

Inspiration Drawing — Page 126

INTRODUCTION

In presenting these drawings and photographs it is proper to include a brief history of the Shakers, since all their designs of the buildings and artifacts were subordinate to their religious beliefs and established laws. The architectural designs — which are distinctive — evolved within the Shaker community and established a style, or a folk art in America.

A group of English Quakers led by James and Jane Wardley in Manchester, England, who had adopted some of the beliefs of the French Prophets, or Camisards of Vivarais and Dauphine, gave to the world a new religion which was to be known as the Shakers, or Believers in Christ's Second Appearing.

In 1758, Ann Lee (1736-1784), an illiterate woman, who was the daughter of a local blacksmith, joined this group and soon thereafter was proclaimed as the anointed one and replaced the Wardleys as leader. She was regarded as the female expression of the Christ Spirit, and Jesus of Nazareth as the male expression of that spirit.

In 1774, while a prisoner in the Manchester jail for breaking the Sabbath by her noisy songs and shouts, she reported to her followers upon her release that she had received a visit from Jesus who directed her to take her followers to the North American Colonies, where they would be able to practice and propagate their faith unmolested. This was accomplished through the generosity of John Hocknell (1723-1799), a member who had funds, and who agreed to pay for the voyage of those who cared to sail for North America.

Only nine persons chose to venture across the Atlantic on the old and unsafe ship, the *Mariah*. They left England on May 19, 1774, and by some miracle arrived in New York on Sunday afternoon, August 6, 1774. After a short residence in New York City, where the members followed various occupations, they decided to change their home to a secluded place.

John Hocknell went to Albany, New York, and acquired land in the wilderness in Niskayuna (now known as West Albany or Watervliet) from Squire Stephen Van Rensselaer, Lord of the Manor of Rensselaerwyck. Here the Shakers cleared and drained the swamp lands, and built log cabins. It was here they suffered physical privation from hunger and cold, but they were free to practice their religious beliefs without interference.

It was not until Joseph Meacham, Talmadge Bishop, and Calvin Harlow — who were the leaders of a group of revivalists at Mount Lebanon, New York — went to Niskayuna to investigate the Believers' faith that the general public began hearing about the "Shaking Quakers." This group of revivalists again sent their emissaries to Niskayuna to investigate and, like Meacham, Bishop, and Harlow, returned to Mount Lebanon to declare that it was the most satisfying of all faiths they had known, and that these Shakers were the true disciples of the faith they had long sought.

Mother Ann Lee, and Father William Lee (1743-1784), a brother of Mother Ann, went to Mount Lebanon on invitation to tell of their beliefs and to preach their gospel. This was, in fact, the beginning of a proselyting journey in New York and the New England states that took them to thirty-six towns. Men and women "gathered in like doves"; husbands and wives and their children embraced this new faith, and those divided in opinion separated and went their own way.

It was this separation of the families and the Shaker preachment of the celibate life that brought persecution and prosecution to the group. Their enemies accused them of trying to annihilate the human race and of being English spies. The leaders, including Mother Ann, were thrown into the jails of Albany and Poughkeepsie but were freed when no just reason for their imprisonment was established. In 1784, both Mother Ann Lee (1743-1784), and Father William Lee (1736-1784), died as a result of mob attacks upon them on a trip through New England. Their deaths were deemed as sacrifices for the faith, and the converts determined to establish their faith more firmly.

The cardinal principles of Shakerism were celibacy, community of goods, confession of sins, and withdrawal from the world. On these principles, the pioneers and those who followed them built their own environment — Paradise on earth.

The Shaker Society was organized at Mount Lebanon, New York, in 1788. It was here that the members came to live in a community where they could worship and work together, and be free from the interference of the world's people. Within this community the Millennial Laws were formulated by Father Joseph Meacham, the first American convert, and Mother Lucy Wright. These laws explained what was and what was not in the Gospel Order, for both personal conduct and communal administration. These laws guided not only the Mount Lebanon Society, but also all the societies established thereafter.

There were nineteen Shaker Societies established in the United States, and just before the Civil War the membership numbered about six thousand.

The Shaker government was vested in Christ and in his human representatives, a dual order of leaders. The ministry consisted of brethren and sisters whose special duty was to guide and superintend the spiritual concerns of the Society, and to cooperate with the elders and eldresses, who protected the spiritual affairs of their own families. The temporal affairs were cared for by the trustees, deacons and deaconesses. All of these leaders were accountable to the Central Ministry, which was located at the Church Family, Mount Lebanon, New York.

From 1790 to just before the Civil War, within the Shaker Society, manufacturing, agriculture and invention were at their greatest height. Agricultural products were produced in such abundance that the trustees were forced to find a market for those commodities which exceeded home consumption. Shaker brethren, therefore, were familiar figures selling their wares in the local market places, the streets of the cities, towns and villages near Shaker settlements.

Their garden seed business, begun about 1789, made them the first to commercialize this product. This was one of the most lucrative businesses carried on in several of the Shaker communities. This business passed out of existence when the world's business men entered the field with great financial investments and advertising.

At Mount Lebanon, New York, the medicinal herb business was started about 1800. Under the leadership of competent botanists, Brother Elias Harlow and Brother Barnabas Hinckley, this business grew rapidly. Not only were herbs assorted and packaged, but extracts, powders, essential oils, salves, syrup compounds, and pills were sold all over the world to druggists and physicians.

Many other products were made in the Shaker shops in the various communities, such as tinware for dairy and kitchen uses, leather shoes, boots, harnesses, and hats. From the sisters' shops came such products as all kinds of woolen cloth, linen cloth, fans, cloaks, canned fruits and vegetables, and also baskets. To this list could be added many other products.

Shaker oval boxes and chairs epitomize Shaker plainness and beauty. The beauty was created by making these objects "functional," because starting out to design a beautiful object was "not in order"; in the Shaker view beauty was a snare of the devil, and the Millennial Laws forbade the Believers to create beauty for beauty's sake.

The oval boxes were general utility boxes and often came in nests of twelve, the smallest being about three inches long and two inches high, and the largest about fifteen inches long and eight inches high. They were made of maple and pine.

The chairs, both straight chairs and rockers, were of a simple New England slat-back type. The rockers were made with and without arms. The straight chairs, sometimes called "tilting chairs," had the rear post terminating with a pine cone finial, without imitation carving. The rear post of most of the "tilting" chairs was fitted with a special Shaker invention — the ball and socket in the lower rear post. The ball, flattened on the floor end, was attached in the socket by leather thongs. This device, known among the Shakers as a "Casidomia" (derived from the Spanish—casi—almost, and domia—asleep) prevented slipping and also damaging the floor or carpet. The South Family at Mount Lebanon, New York, were known as the champion chairmakers of the world (Manifesto, July 1895).

There are many inventions known to be of Shaker origin, and many others are in use today but not generally attributed to these people. A few of the common objects of Shaker invention in use today are metallic pens, clothespins, apple-parers, one-horse wagons, and flat corn brooms. It was Sister Tabitha Babbit, of the Harvard, Massachusetts, Society, who is accredited with the invention of the circular saw. ("Gleaning from Old Shaker Journals" by Clara E. Sears, 1916; *"Simonds Guide for Millmen,"* Simonds Manufacturing Company, Vol. XIV, No. 2, March-April 1922.)

As late as sixty years ago it was not an uncommon sight to see the Shaker sisters and brethren walking through the streets of nearby cities and villages; as in Albany, New York; Harvard, Massachusetts; Concord, New Hampshire, and Pittsfield, Massachusetts. They had many business errands to perform in these places, where they solicited and delivered orders for products of the Shaker farms and shops. They were identifiable by their dress.

The sisters wore long dresses with wide pleated skirts, and a plain bodice, over which was draped a cotton or silk neckerchief which was folded and pinned at the belt to form a bertha. The head covering was a poke bonnet of woven straw, or of quilted cloth. A cape, about five inches broad and made of a thin cloth, was sewn to the back edge of this bonnet, to protect the neck from the sun in summer and from the cold in winter.

During the colder months of the year the sisters wore a circular cape fitted with a hood that covered the bonnet if desired. These capes were made of gray, black, and brown broadcloth.

The original costume for women was adopted from the antique style in vogue at the time of the inception of the organization. The designing of this original uniform has been attributed to Mother Lucy Wright, but changes in this attire have been made during the past seventy years.

The brethren's costume for working in the shops and in the fields consisted of loose trousers and a smock of unbleached or bleached coarse linen. The hats, all Shaker-made, were broad-brimmed with high crowns. For Sundays the suits were made of fine woven materials of wool, or wool-and-cotton mixture. A vest was worn over a white shirt, and over this a long frock coat of the same color or of a lighter hue. The winter overcoat, or surtout, was a fitted long coat with a shoulder cape. The colors of these coats were gray, dark blue, tan, or black.

In 1849, Elder Harvey L. Eads of South Union, Kentucky, published his *"Tailor's Division System,"* illustrated with eighteen plates and three additional plates of diagrams, which made for a more uniform dress among the brethren.

The shoes for both brethren and sisters were made by the Shaker cobblers, and usually had handwoven cloth tops with leather heels and soles.

Many theories have been projected as to the cause of the decline of the Shaker organization, or Believers in Christ's Second Appearing, but certainly no single one of them can be accepted as conclusive. To those not familiar with the social and economic history of this period, the celibate restrictions placed upon Shaker members would naturally seem to be the one and only reason. Celibacy was not even the dominant reason, but it was, without any doubt, a contributing factor. The Believers approved of marriage and procreation for the world's people but not for themselves, for they were of a higher spiritual order and intended to follow the life of Jesus Christ, whose life was one of continence.

During and after the Civil War there was a sharp decline in the membership, especially among the male population. During the war young men and women, who might have joined the Shaker Society, entered into other pursuits; the young men joined the Army, and the young women entered into business or industry. After the war the rapid industrialization that took place in the North, the South, and the West lured men and women into the factories and offices; the trek westward from the east in search of gold and homesteading, also drew prospective members from the Shaker fold.

The "deserving female" converts no longer swelled the ranks as they had twenty years before the Young Women's Christian Association in New York City opened a training class in typewriting for young women. Classes in other cities were opened and soon "the female typewriters" were in demand. The social stigma against working women was abolished, and young women and widows left alone in the world went into offices to earn an independent living — they no longer sought the Shakers for protection and security.

Men and women who had been in the Shaker Society withdrew at an alarming rate because they no longer had the "calling" for the Shaker way of life. And, too, state laws were instituted which regulated the adoptions and education of children, and the establishing of orphan asylums by other religious groups and governments diminished the numbers taken into the "Children's Order." The Shakers not only enjoyed having children to care for and train, but hoped that many would stay among them when they reached the age of twenty-one years and would then choose to sign the Covenant of their own volition.

All Shaker societies suffered during the Civil War, especially those in Kentucky, which never recovered from the loss sustained from the marauding Union and Confederate troops. The northern societies stood by and saw their once large and lucrative enterprises shrink and disappear before their eyes. The very industries, which they had started shortly after their organization in 1788, were taken by the "world's people" who had large funds to invest and were willing to take a gambler's chance in order to reap large financial returns with cheap labor, machinery and extensive advertising. The investors were rewarded with large profits. The Shakers could not compete with the low selling prices of the finished machine products of the outside manufacturer.

Some members blamed the friction that took place in the organization as the fatal blow. The fission separated the group into two parts, which weakened the structure of the Society. A conservative group headed by Elder Harvey Eads of Kentucky and Elder Henry Blinn of the New Hampshire group believed that the Shaker should adhere strictly to the principles of Mother Ann Lee in regard to living apart from the world's people. On the other side of the chasm was the liberal group led by Elder Frederick Evans of Mount Lebanon, New York, who advocated that Shakers should take an active part in world affairs. Evans and his liberal group dominated, thus creating an organization divided against itself. Elder Frederick grew more obdurate as he grew older and had things his way until his last days.

A middle group arose and was led by Eldress Lelia Taylor and Eldress Anna White, but the fissure could not be closed—it was too wide and too deep.

In later years the business affairs of the Shaker Society were greatly harmed by mismanagement by those who had taken over. The Shakers were not properly prepared to assume responsibility, since they had not been trained to the revolutionary changes that had taken place in the world's business and commerce, and consequently suffered great financial losses.

Summing up all of these social and economic changes that have brought to near-extermination the oldest of the socio-religious groups in the United States, it can only be said that the Shakers have made great contributions to the United States and to civilization. Marguerite Fellows Melcher, author of *The Shaker Adventure,* states in a letter to the writer that "Everything in this world — from flowers to civilization — seems to fade, decline from its moment of most perfect fulfillment. Why? Maybe it is a law of the universe."

Nineteen Shaker Societies were established in the United States, and during their heyday there were about six thousand members. Today there are two Societies left: one at Canterbury, New Hampshire, and the other at

Sabbath Day Lake, Maine. The total membership is twenty-two. There are no living Brethren.

During the great "ingathering" of members and communal prosperity, which occurred between 1790-1864, all Shaker settlements launched an overwhelming building program. During this time new dwelling houses and shops were erected or old ones remodeled for the convenience and comfort of the increasing membership. With combined efforts of the master builders, masons, stonecutters, bricklayers, lumber workers, and blacksmiths those buildings that are still standing were constructed according to the Gospel Order, or the rules concerning building set down in the Millennial Laws.

At this time the Shakers had among them men of much experience in construction work. From the Shaker *Manifesto,* the monthly journal, autobiographies and biographies, research discloses that "master builders," or architects, possessed extraordinary ability, and what is left for inspection attests to this claim. Elder Giles Avery at Mount Lebanon, New York, was a famed carpenter; Elder Harvey Eads of South Union, Kentucky, was not only a skilled carpenter, but a most versatile man in other trades as well. Micajah Burnett at Pleasant Hills was an experienced architect and builder before joining the Shakers, as was Elder Moses Johnson of Enfield, New Hampshire, who was a master builder of Meeting Houses. Added to this list was Elder George Wickersham who, as a youth, and before joining the Shakers, was a builder.

The buildings at Mount Lebanon, New York, served as models for other communities established later. Master builders from the Shaker village at Mount Lebanon often went to the newly-established settlements to supervise and assist in the construction work of newly-formed communities.

In the dwelling houses were the "retiring rooms" (or bedrooms), the kitchens, bake-rooms, food storage rooms and dining rooms. Here also was the "Meetings Room," where the "family" assembled in the evening for a religious service; to discuss the business and work program for the next day, and to hear a report on world affairs by those who had been assigned to read the current newspapers and periodicals. This room was equipped with either chairs or benches and was usually located on the first floor, but sometimes on the second floor.

The retiring rooms were on the first floor and the floors above. Each room was spacious enough to accommodate from three to four single beds. Built-in or movable chests of draws and cupboards were ample to accommodate the belongings of those who occupied a room. Adjoining each retiring room was a dressing room in which there were several "wash-sinks" with their own bowls and pitcher sets, towel racks, and peg boards for hanging up clothing.

In the basement were the dining rooms for the family and the guests. The large family dining room was entered by separate doors for the sisters and brethren. They sat at separate tables and at opposite ends of the room, near their respective entrances. Around the room, as in every other room, was a row of peg boards, on which each person hung his or her chair at the conclusion of each meal. This facilitated the cleaning of the tables and floors by those in charge of the dining room. The built-in cupboards and chests of drawers were ample to accommodate the large quantities of china, glass, silverware and linens. In the dining room, near the china cupboards, was a sink with drainboards for washing glass, china, and silverware used at meal times.

Adjoining the dining room was the kitchen, separated by a double door to allow free passage for those who replenished the serving dishes. Both doors remained open during the meal hours.

The location of the kitchen range determined the placing of other conveniences, such as tables, counters, shelves, and sinks. The cook's counter was opposite the stove. The top half near the dining room was made of wood; the other half, near the kitchen sink, was stone. The wooden portion of the top was for the serving dishes; and the stone portion for pots and pans that could be lifted directly from the stove. In this way there was no damage to chinaware, and no burning of the table top from pots and pans.

A counter near the cooling room, or refrigerator room, was the spot to which the left-over food from the dining room was returned. Cupboards under this counter, or nearby, accommodated the vessels used for storing the left-over food from the dining room and kitchen. A few steps from this counter was the "cooling-room."

The cooling room was paved with slabs of marble or blue flagstone. Here were tables with stone tops, and stone basins partly filled with water in which crocks or earthenware containers with food were placed. Basins of stone held large blocks of ice or, as in the case of the room in the North Family, Mount Lebanon, New York, water from the springs in the mountain which circulated through pipes that surrounded the walls. No ice was required in this room.

The bake-room on the same floor and often adjoining the kitchen had its own especially designed brick oven, arch kettles, and sinks. There were a few standing pieces, such as wooden and stone-top tables, flour bins, and tables for cutting bread. Conveniently placed on the walls were hanging cupboards and shelves for supplies. Adjacent to this room was a pan and supply room.

The canning and preserving kitchen with its storeroom was remote from the other kitchen and bake-rooms. It too was equipped with special arch kettles, sinks, counters, tables, hanging cupboards for condiments, and small equipment used in canning. The storeroom for the canned goods was under this kitchen, which made it possible to have a "lift" or dumbwaiter from the kitchen to this subterranean room. The jars and crocks with preserved food were placed on stone-topped tables or on counters placed around the room, which was rodent-and insect-proof. The floor, paved with slabs of bluestone at a depth below ground was always cool during the warmest days of summer.

The attics of all Shaker dwelling houses were completely finished. Some of them were divided into rooms and had built-in cases of drawers and cupboards.

The floors, if not in a natural finish, were stained a reddish yellow, and the floor boards were narrow or wide, depending on the era in which the building was erected.

The walls were plain plaster and painted white, or cerulean blue, which is often called "Shaker blue"; some were light tan. The woodwork in the room was a natural finish or ochre yellow.

It will be noted upon inspection of the drawings that because of the physical location of kitchens, dining rooms, bake-rooms, and storerooms, there was no reason for the workers to leave the confines of their respective working areas.

The shops, of course, showed greater variations in plan than the dwelling houses. Designed for particular occupations, they necessarily differed in arrangement. Workbenches and storage cabinets were placed so as to avoid lost motion by the artisan and to provide him with a maximum of comfort and safety. The location of a shop within a building was always carefully planned. If the occupation required a hoist or an elevator such was placed in the room, or nearby, in order to reduce handling; whether the doors were double or off center, was also determined by the bulk of the raw material to be brought in and the size of the finished products going out.

The exteriors of all buildings were plain and well proportioned, without embellishment that added nothing to the structural purity which gave eminence to Shaker architecture. All structures in a Shaker village, both inside and outside, reflected the lives of the people who lived and worked in them.

The great barns at Canterbury, New Hampshire; Mount Lebanon, New York; Pittsfield (Hancock), Massachusetts, and Watervliet (Niskayuna) New York, upon examination show that much labor and forethought were projected for the care and treatment of the farm animals. The Millennial Law, Section VII, No. 4 was obeyed in planning all Shaker barns for "No beast belonging to the people of God may be left to suffer with hunger, thirst, or cold, in consequence of neglect, on the part of those who have the care of them, but all should be kept in proper places and properly attended to according to their needs."

The silos, grain bins and hay mows were filled to provide bountiful supply for all animals over the most prolonged period from summer to spring. The construction of barns was tight and properly ventilated, and every device possible was made to insure a clean and sanitary condition. The architectural drawings of the barns at the North Family, Mount Lebanon, New York, and the "round" barn at Pittsfield, Massachusetts, show this.

The reader's attention is called to the use made of the hillsides in constructing a barn and other structures. By taking advantage of the natural topography, the various levels of a barn could be entered easily into and without bridges, which were expensive to build as well as to maintain.

Since they were chiefly an agrarian group, much attention was paid to planning a barn by the master builders.

The architectural drawings reproduced here and supplemented by photographs show a distinctive style of structure that evolved within the Believers' communities. Architectural designs, as all other forms in the community ,were subordinate to the Millennial Laws that guarded the Shaker master builder or architect against any styles or devices he may have employed out in the "world." However, during the last quarter of the nineteenth century when the Shaker male population was greatly reduced outside builders were hired to assist in construction work, especially when the project was too enormous for the brethren to undertake alone. Deviations from pure Shaker buildings are noticed where outside builders were employed. Outstanding examples are the dwelling house and the Ministry's residence at the Church Family, Mount Lebanon, New York, erected after the great fire of 1875.

In Kentucky, regional differences in architecture are reflected in some of the buildings. However, the majority of these structures are basically Shaker-influenced.

There are many unique features about Shaker buildings that made them different from others. The interior wall treatment, the floor and woodwork, the windows, the ubiquitous peg boards, the stair rails, doors, hardware, door canopies without external supports, hand rails, boot scrapers on the steps, and the plain but beautiful exterior gave charm not only to a building but to the entire Shaker community. Even today, when the buildings are occupied by groups alien to the Shaker belief, there is a great spiritual feeling of peace that pervades an entire Shaker village.

The drawings herewith presented were produced by the Works Progress Administration's New York State Museum Project Number 50470, during the economic recession of 1929-1941. The late Charles C. Adams, Director of the New York State Museum, and Andrew Delahanty, Supervisor of the United States Government Historical Building Survey, selected the buildings to be measured because they were the most representative and important structures left in the Shaker communities at Watervliet, Albany County, New York; Mount Lebanon, Columbia County, New York; and Pittsfield (West Pittsfield or Hancock), Berkshire County, Massachusetts. A few of these buildings that were measured during the survey are no longer extant, and many of those existing have undergone changes to meet the requirements of the present owners. These vicissitudes, combined with disuse and the destructive forces of the natural elements, have in many cases played havoc in these once model Shaker communities.

Collections of Shaker materials and literature are to be found in the New York State Library at Albany, New York; Western Reserve Historical Society, Cleveland, Ohio; Shaker Heights Historical Society, and the Shaker Heights Savings Association at Shaker Heights, Ohio; Golden Lamb Inn, Lebanon, Ohio; Dartmouth College Museum and Library at Hanover, New Hampshire; Fruitlands and Wayside Museum, Harvard, Massachusetts; Shaker Museum, Old Chatham, New York; Williams College Library, Williamstown, Massachusetts; Grosvenor Library, Buffalo, New York; New York Public Library, New York; The Library of Congress, Washington, District of Columbia; School of Religion, State University of Iowa, Iowa City, Iowa; Francis DuPont Winterthur Museum, Winterthur, Delaware; Hancock Shaker Village, Hancock, Massachusetts; Shaker Museum, Auburn, Kentucky; Pleasant Hill at Old Shakertown Incorporated, Shakertown, Kentucky, and the New York State Museum at Albany.

The watercolor renderings of the Shaker objects made by the Works Progress Administration's artist between 1927-1937 are in the Federal Index of Design, National Art Gallery, Washington, D. C. The architectural drawings and the photographs used in this publication are in the collections of the Historic American Building Survey, Library of Congress, Washington, D.C. These are of great importance to research students, especially those interested in Shaker folk arts and designs.

Many thanks are given to Professor Lionel Wyld, Dr. Frederick H. Bair, Miss Estella Weeks, Mrs. Ethel Hotaling Drumm, and Mrs. Marguerite Fellows Melcher for their help and invaluable criticism.

I am indebted to the Library of Congress for the use of the architectural drawings and the photographs from the permanent collections, all of which were made under the Works Progress Administration 1929-1941.

To Constantine Kermes who made the illustrations for this book, and Mrs. Marion Bollman Bender who handled the typing of the manuscript, I am most grateful.

William Lawrence Lassiter

Albany, New York, 1962

The Stone Barn

*STONE BARN: NORTH FAMILY, MOUNT
LEBANON, NEW YORK*

The great stone barn was completed in 1858, under the supervision of
Elder George Wickersham, the designer. His original plans of this building
(New York State Museum's Historical Catalog Number 6248) are in the
Shaker Collection at the New York State Museum.

The dimensions are 196 feet long by 50 feet wide. There are five floors
in all, three of which — the first, second and fourth — may be entered by
doors that open at their level on the hillside, thus eliminating bridges. The
original flat roof was removed some years after construction and replaced by
a gable roof covered with slate, to prevent the accumulation of snow which
would have added to the weight.

Stone Barn

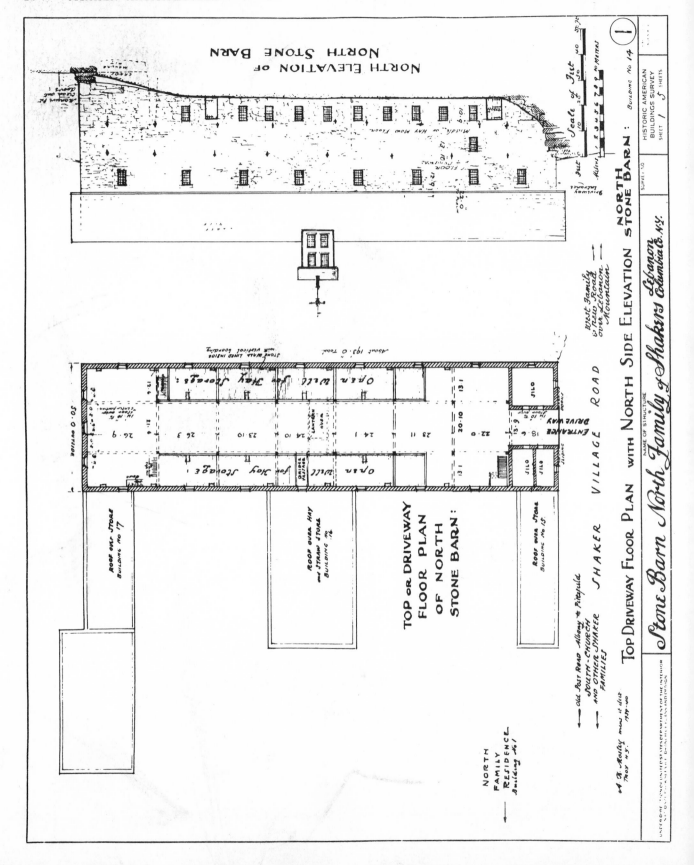

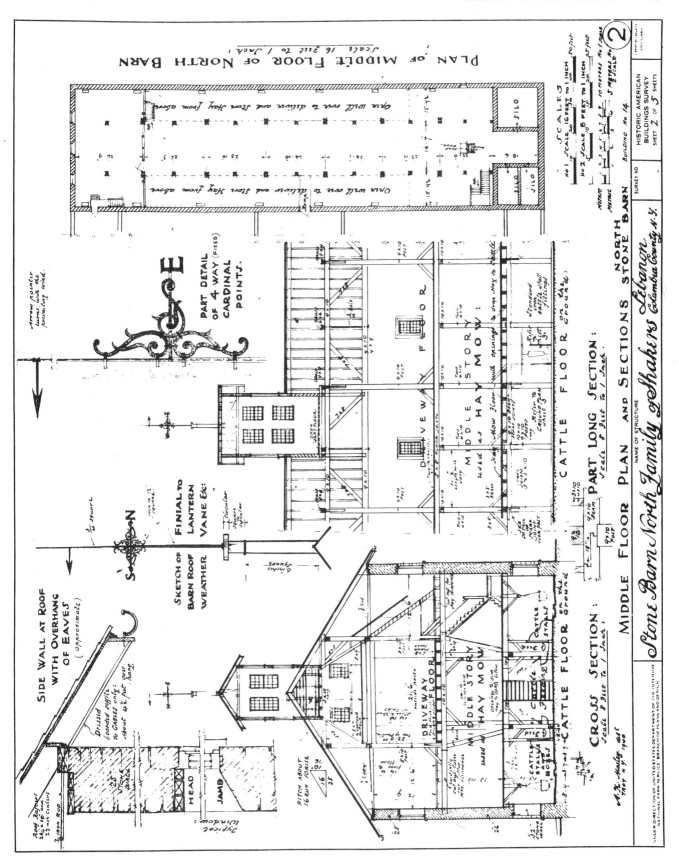

PLAN OF MIDDLE FLOOR OF NORTH BARN

Scale 16 feet to 1 Inch;

SCALES

HISTORIC AMERICAN BUILDINGS SURVEY
SHEET 2 OF 5 SHEETS

BUILDING No. 14.

SIDE WALL AT ROOF WITH OVERHANG OF EAVES (approximate)

SKETCH OF BARN ROOF WEATHER

FINIAL TO LANTERN VANE &c:

PART DETAIL OF 4 WAY (FIXED) CARDINAL POINTS.

MIDDLE WAY HAY STORY

DRIVE WAY FLOOR

CATTLE FLOOR ON THE GROUND

PART LONG SECTION:
Scale 8 feet to 1 Inch.

CROSS SECTION:
Scale 8 feet to 1 Inch.

MIDDLE FLOOR PLAN AND SECTIONS
NORTH STONE BARN

Stone Barn North Family of Shakers Lebanon
Columbia County, N.Y.

A.H. Harley, del.
Troy N.Y. 1940

On the lower floor, west elevation, the refuse pits are located; this made it possible for wagons to be driven in and out through the two broad doorways.

On the east end lies the entrance to the fourth floor from the main Shaker road. The large sliding doors admitted a team of horses with a loaded hayrack. At the west end of this floor space was arranged so that the team, after unloading the hayrack into the self-leveling hay mow, could turn around and leave by the same east door through which the team had entered. At this entrance, on the east end and on both sides, are the openings for filling the built-in silos.

On the south side are attached wooden buildings, open cattle sheds, and sheds for farm implements, which project into a fenced cattle yard.

This structure is reputed to be the largest all-stone barn in the United States.

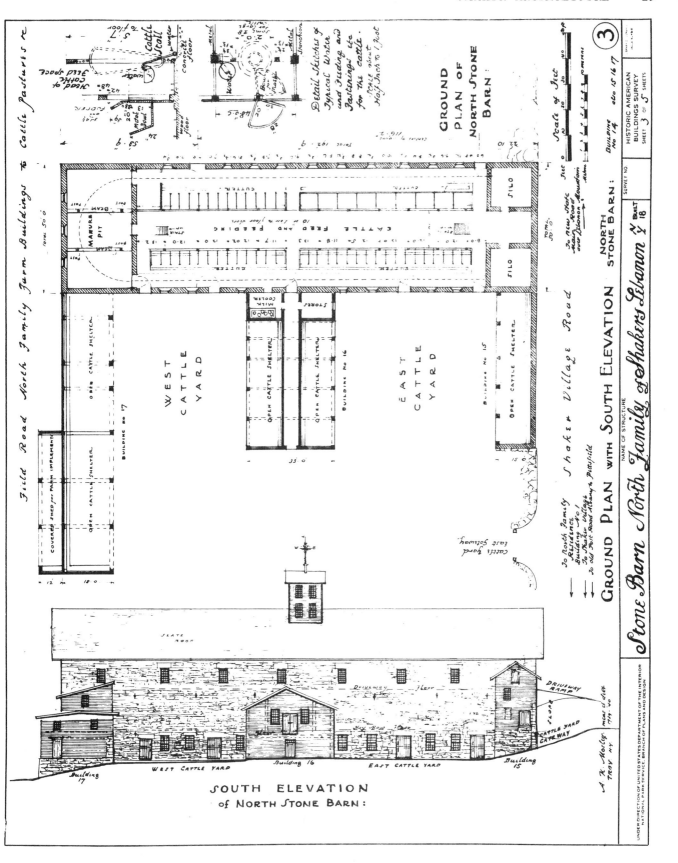

SHAKER ARCHITECTURE — 29

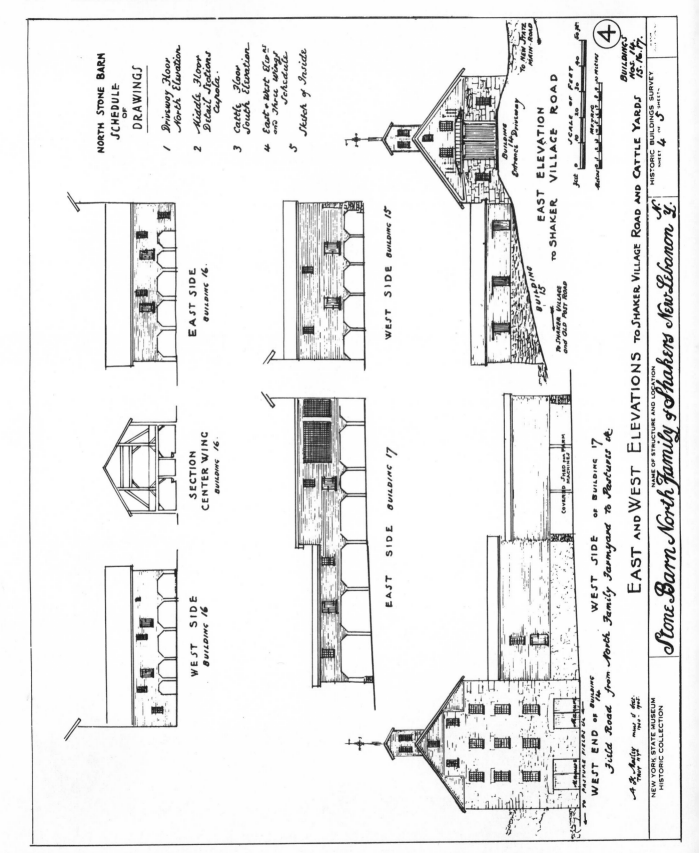

NORTH STONE BARN
SCHEDULE
of
DRAWINGS

1   Driveway Floor
    North Elevation

2   Middle Floor
    Detail Sections
    Cupola.

3   Cattle Floor
    South Elevation.

4   East + West Elev.
    and Three Wings
    Schedule

5   Sketch of Inside

EAST SIDE
BUILDING 16

SECTION
CENTER WING
BUILDING 16.

WEST SIDE BUILDING 15

WEST SIDE
BUILDING 16

EAST SIDE BUILDING 17

BUILDING
15

To NEW STATE MAIN ROAD

Building Entrance & Driveway

EAST ELEVATION
To SHAKER VILLAGE ROAD

To SHAKER VILLAGE
and OLD PLATT ROAD

SCALE or FEET

COVERED SHED for FARM MACHINERY

WEST END of BUILDING 16
WEST SIDE of BUILDING 17
Field Road from North Family Farmyard to Pastures &c.

← To PASTURE FIELDS &c.

A.H. Autig del.
Troy N.Y.

EAST and WEST ELEVATIONS To SHAKER VILLAGE ROAD and CATTLE YARDS

Stone Barn North Family of Shakers New Lebanon Y.

NAME OF STRUCTURE AND LOCATION

HISTORIC BUILDINGS SURVEY
SHEET 4 of 5 SHEETS

BUILDINGS
NOS. 14.
15. 16. 17.

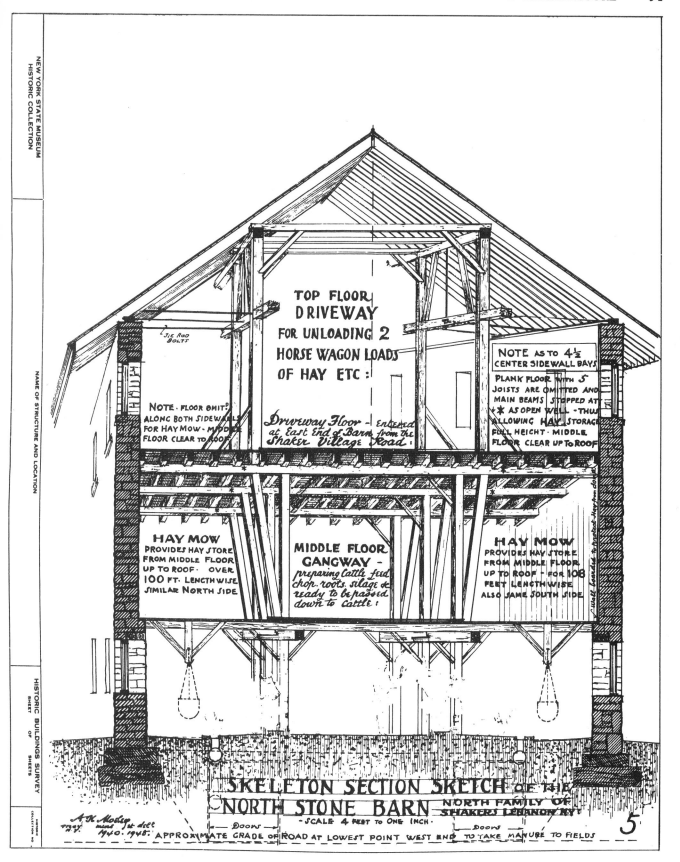

TIE ROD BOLTS

TOP FLOOR
DRIVEWAY
FOR UNLOADING 2
HORSE WAGON LOADS
OF HAY ETC:

NOTE · FLOOR OMIT?
ALONG BOTH SIDEWALLS
FOR HAY MOW · MIDDLE
FLOOR CLEAR TO ROOF

Driveway Floor — Entered
at East End of Barn from the
Shaker Village Road:

NOTE AS TO 4½
CENTER SIDEWALL BAYS

PLANK FLOOR WITH 5"
JOISTS ARE OMITTED AND
MAIN BEAMS STOPPED AT
+ ✱ AS OPEN WELL — THUS
ALLOWING HAY STORAGE
FULL HEIGHT · MIDDLE
FLOOR CLEAR UP TO ROOF

HAY MOW
PROVIDES HAY STORE
FROM MIDDLE FLOOR
UP TO ROOF · OVER
100 FT · LENGTHWISE
SIMILAR NORTH SIDE

MIDDLE FLOOR
GANGWAY —
preparing cattle feed
chop. roots. silage &
ready to be passed
down to cattle :

HAY MOW
PROVIDES HAY STORE
FROM MIDDLE FLOOR.
UP TO ROOF · FOR 108
FEET LENGTHWISE
ALSO SAME SOUTH SIDE

SKELETON SECTION SKETCH OF THE
NORTH STONE BARN NORTH FAMILY OF
SHAKERS LEBANON N.Y.
· SCALE 4 FEET TO ONE INCH ·

A.H. Mosle
N.Y. meas. ft. del.
1940 · 1948 · APPROXIMATE GRADE OF ROAD AT LOWEST POINT WEST END TO TAKE MANURE TO FIELDS

DOORS   DOORS

5

DWELLING HOUSE: NORTH FAMILY,
MOUNT LEBANON, NEW YORK

A five-story basement and subbasement building, this dwelling was erected in 1818. The north end was added in 1846.

Like many Shaker buildings, this house was constructed in order to take advantage of the topography. The south subbasement has the furnace room, store room, brethren's wash room, and a storage room. The north subbasement has the cold cellars for the storage of preserved foods.

The basement, which is one flight down from the main east entrance, accommodates the kitchens, bakery, family dining room, guest dining room, hired men's dining room, pantries, store rooms, and the refrigerator room. The cooling or refrigerator room, a forerunner of our modern walk-in refrigerator rooms, is encircled with pipes through which circulated the cold water from a spring-fed reservoir. It served the North Family from the day of its installation to the day the remaining members migrated over the mountain to the Pittsfield Shaker farm in 1947.

In this building are the radiators and the ventilating systems devised by Elder Frederic Evans (1808-1893), noted scholar and Shaker leader.

The windows, doors, hardware, and arch kettles represent excellent examples of Shaker ingenuity and craftsmanship.

Dwelling House

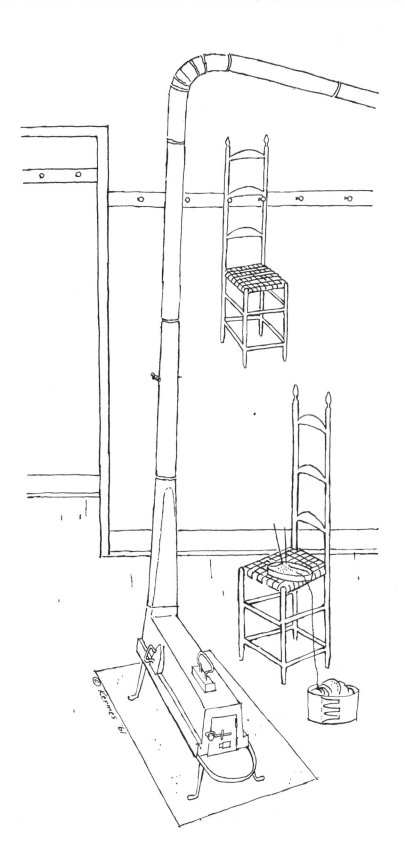

Sister's Room

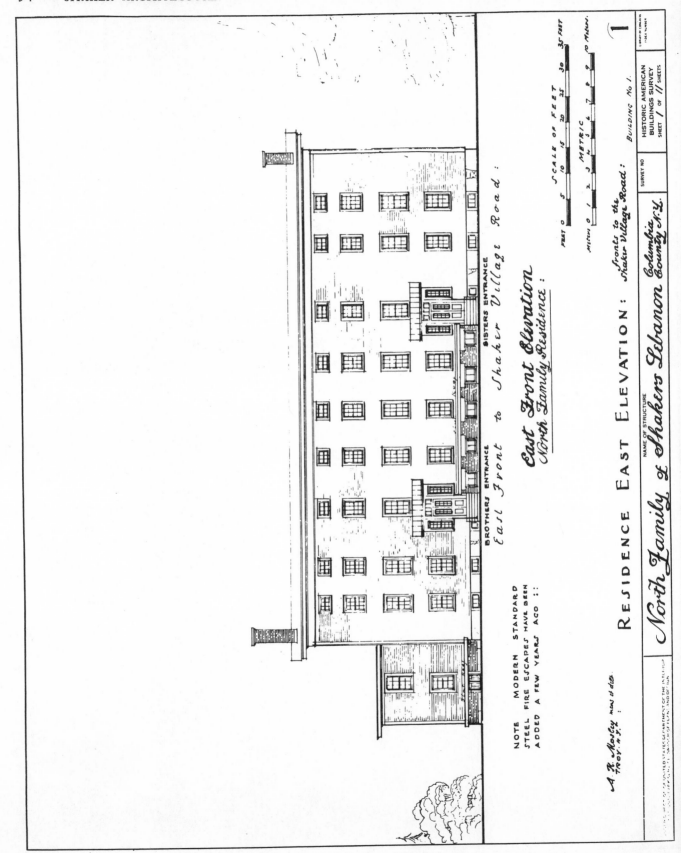

BROTHERS ENTRANCE   SISTERS ENTRANCE

East Front to Shaker Village Road :

East Front Elevation
North Family Residence :

NOTE   MODERN STANDARD
STEEL FIRE ESCAPES HAVE BEEN
ADDED A FEW YEARS AGO ::

A. R. Morley MES & DEL
TROY, N.Y. :

SCALE OF FEET

FEET 0   5   10   15   20   25   30   35 FEET

METRIC

METERS 0   1   2   3   4   5   6   7   8   9   10 METERS

RESIDENCE EAST ELEVATION :   *fronts to the*
Shaker Village Road :

North Family of Shakers Lebanon Columbia County N.Y.

| SURVEY NO | NAME OF STRUCTURE | BUILDING No 1. | |
| HISTORIC AMERICAN BUILDINGS SURVEY SHEET 1 OF 11 SHEETS | | | 1 |

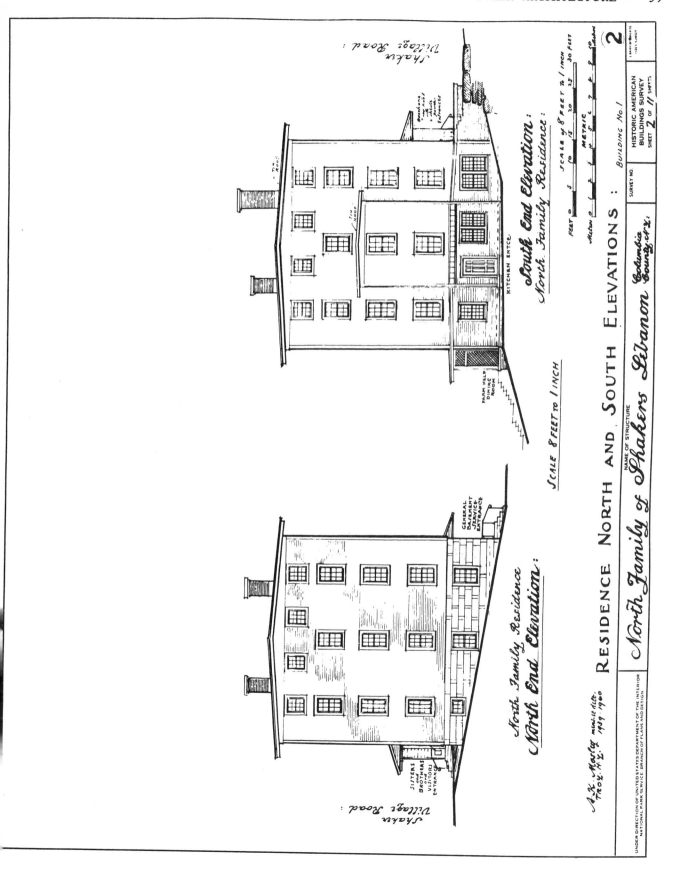

South End Elevation:
North Family Residence:

SCALE 8 FEET to 1 INCH

North Family Residence
North End Elevation:

RESIDENCE NORTH AND SOUTH ELEVATIONS:

North Family of Shakers Lebanon Columbia County, N.Y.

Shaker Village Road:

Shaker Village Road:

KITCHEN ENTCE.

FARM HELP DINING ROOM

GENERAL BASEMENT SERVICE ENTRANCE

SISTERS and BROTHERS and VISITORS ENTRANCE

A.R. Marty delin.1939-1940
TROY. N.Y.

NAME OF STRUCTURE

SURVEY NO   HISTORIC AMERICAN
BUILDINGS SURVEY
BUILDING No.1   SHEET 2 OF 11 SHEETS

UNDER DIRECTION OF UNITED STATES DEPARTMENT OF THE INTERIOR
NATIONAL PARK SERVICE BRANCH OF PLANS AND DESIGN

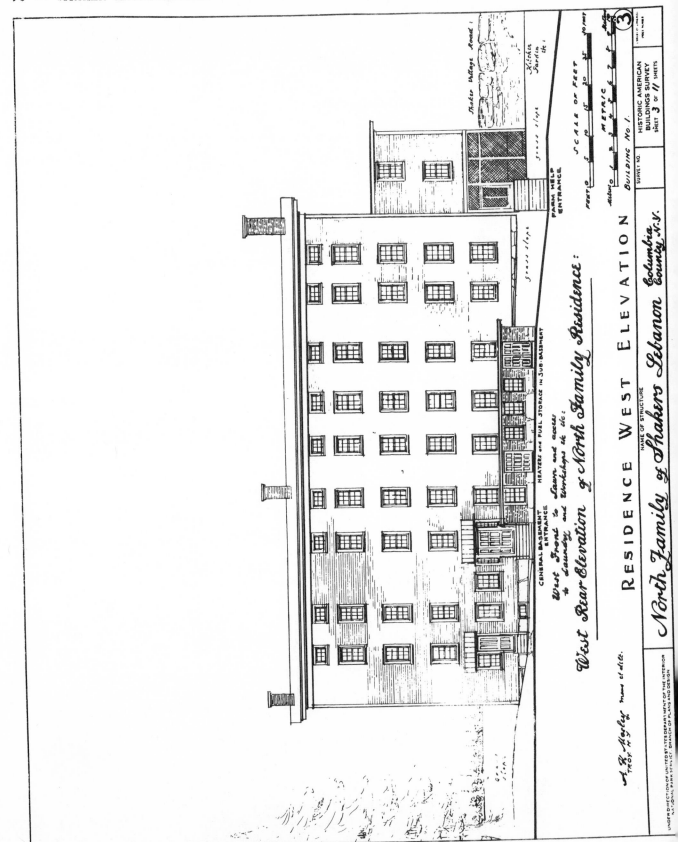

RESIDENCE WEST ELEVATION

West Rear Elevation of North Family Residence:

North Family of Shakers Lebanon Columbia County N.Y.

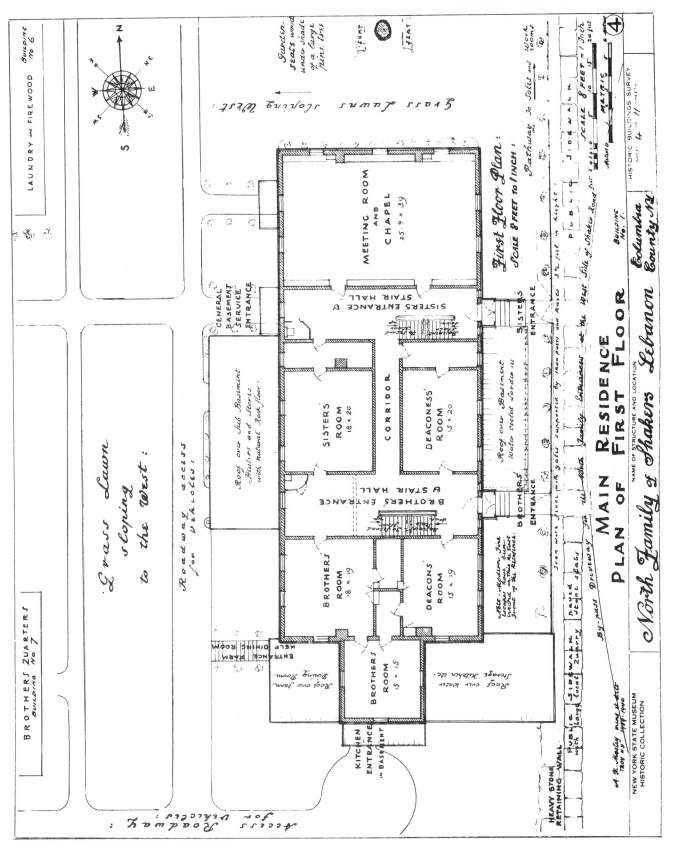

BROTHERS QUARTERS BUILDING No 7

LAUNDRY and FIREWOOD BUILDING No 6

Grass Lawn sloping to the West:

Roadway access for vehicles:

Grass Lawns sloping West:

Seats: wood under shade of a large pine tree.

SEAT

LIGHT

SEAT

MEETING ROOM AND CHAPEL
25'.6 x 39'

SISTERS ENTRANCE & STAIR HALL

BROTHERS ENTRANCE & STAIR HALL

GENERAL BASEMENT SERVICE ENTRANCE

Roof over Sub Basement Heaters and Stores with natural Rock floor:

SISTERS ROOM 18 x 20

CORRIDOR

DEACONESS' ROOM 15 x 20

Roof over Basement Walls coated with tile:

SISTERS ENTRANCE

BROTHERS ROOM 18 x 19

DEACONS' ROOM 15 x 19

BROTHERS ENTRANCE

BROTHERS ROOM 15 x 15

ENTRANCE FARM HELP DINING ROOM

Roof over Jam Storage Rooms:

Roof over Water Storage Kitchen etc.

KITCHEN ENTRANCE in BASEMENT

Access Roadway for vehicles:

First Floor Plan:
SCALE 8 FEET to 1 INCH

Pathway to Walls and Work room:

PUBLIC SIDEWALK

SCALE 8 FEET = 1 Inch

METRIC

HISTORIC BUILDINGS SURVEY
SHEET 4 of 11 SHEETS

Main Residence
PLAN OF FIRST FLOOR
NAME OF STRUCTURE AND LOCATION
North Family of Shakers Lebanon Columbia County N.Y.
BUILDING No. 1.

Iron work fence with gate supported by Iron posts and Rails

By-pass Driveway for the Two Family Entrances at the West side of Shaker Road

PUBLIC SIDEWALK with Large local 2 Story raised Joint Slabs

HEAVY STONE RETAINING WALL

A. R. Hanley mus. State TROY N.Y.

NEW YORK STATE MUSEUM HISTORIC COLLECTION

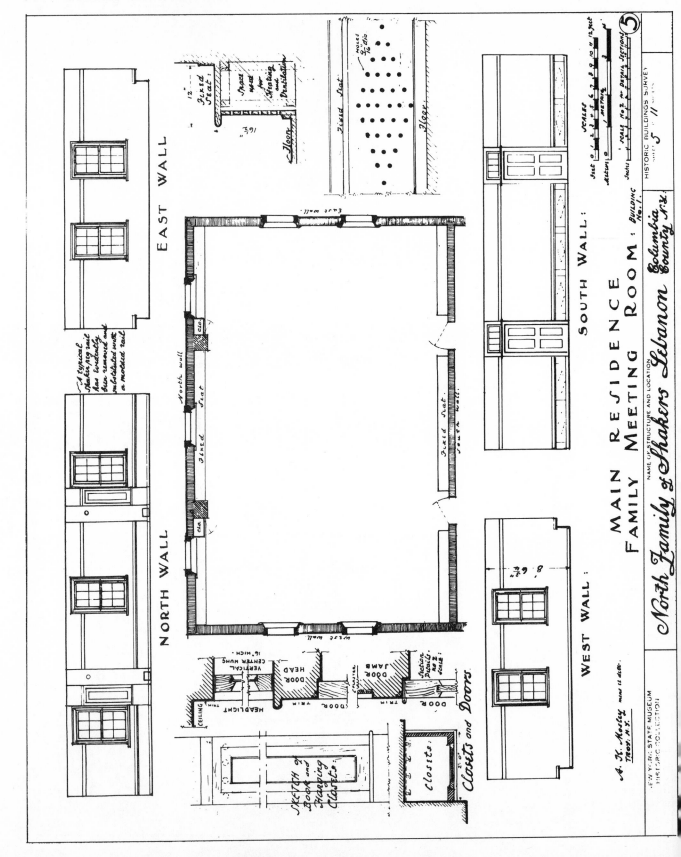

EAST WALL

NORTH WALL

SOUTH WALL:

WEST WALL:

MAIN RESIDENCE
FAMILY MEETING ROOM : BUILDING No. 1.

North Family of Shakers Lebanon Columbia County N.Y.

HISTORIC BUILDINGS SURVEY

A. K. Morley, mea et del.
Troy, N.Y.

NEW YORK STATE MUSEUM
HISTORIC COLLECTION

NAME OF STRUCTURE AND LOCATION

Closets and Doors.

SKETCH of Book and Hanging Closets.

Closets.

Fixed Seat.

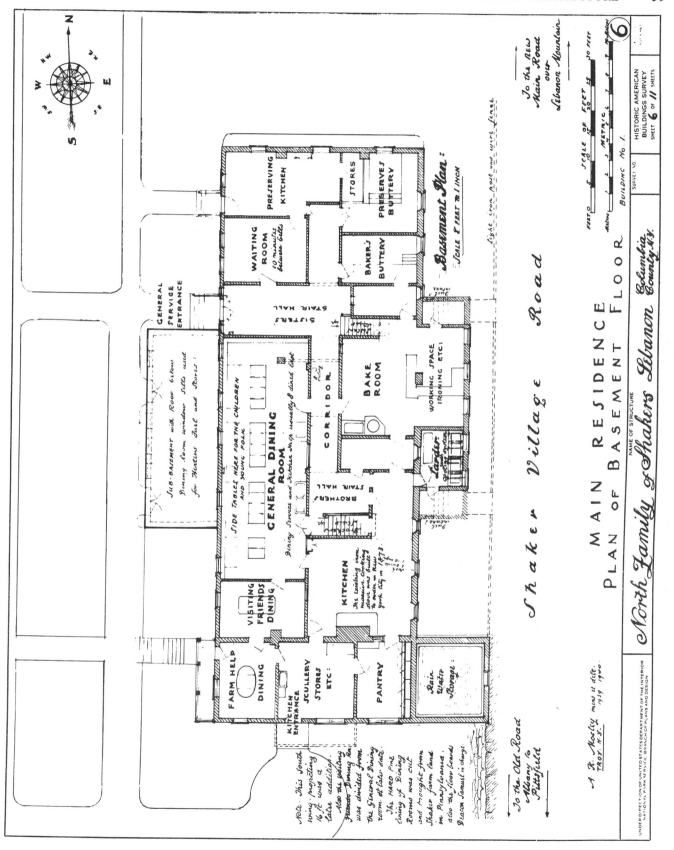

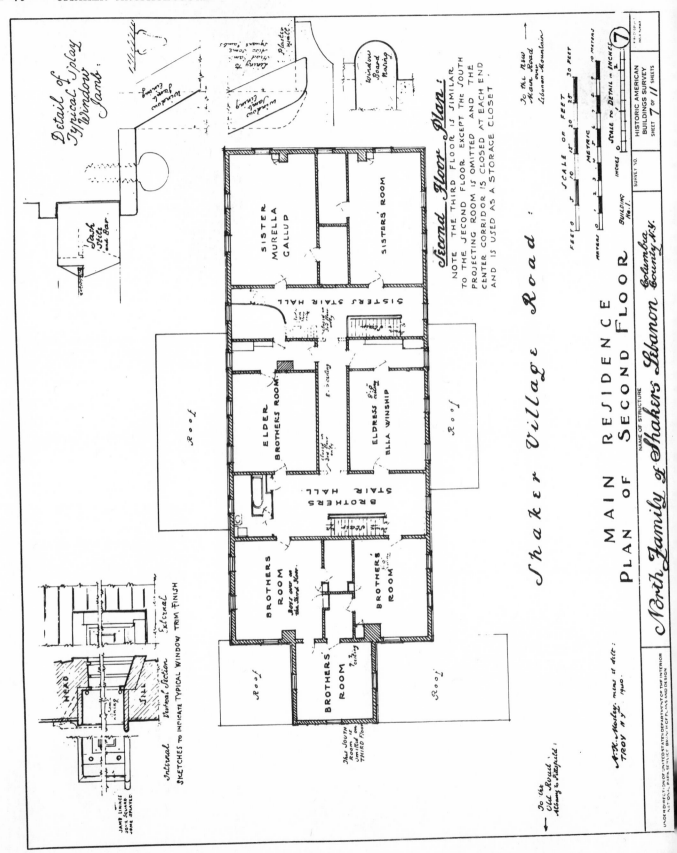

Detail of Typical Splay Window Jamb.

Sketches to indicate typical window trim finish

Internal Vertical Section External

Second Floor Plan:

NOTE THE THIRD FLOOR IS SIMILAR TO THE SECOND FLOOR, EXCEPT THE SOUTH PROJECTING ROOM IS OMITTED AND THE CENTER CORRIDOR IS CLOSED AT EACH END AND IS USED AS A STORAGE CLOSET.

SISTER MURELLA GALLUP

SISTERS' ROOM

SISTERS STAIR HALL

ELDER BROTHERS ROOM

ELDRESS ELLA WINSHIP

BROTHERS STAIR HALL

BROTHERS ROOM

BROTHERS ROOM

BROTHERS ROOM

Roof

Shaker Village Road:

MAIN RESIDENCE
PLAN OF SECOND FLOOR

North Family of Shakers Lebanon, Columbia County, N.Y.

SCALE OF FEET

METRIC

SCALE FOR DETAIL IN INCHES

SURVEY NO.

BUILDING No. 1.

HISTORIC AMERICAN BUILDINGS SURVEY
SHEET 7 of 11 SHEETS

7

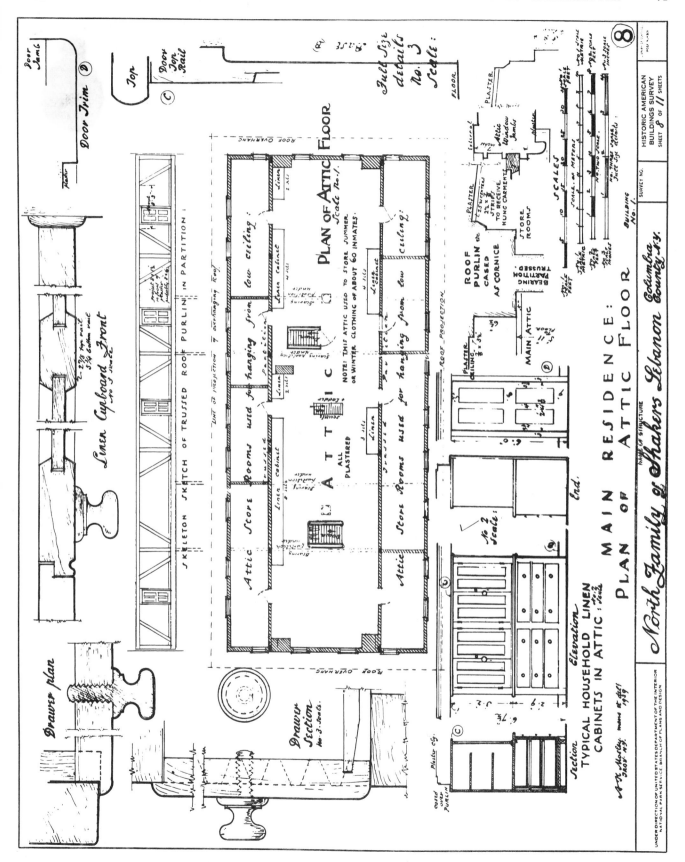

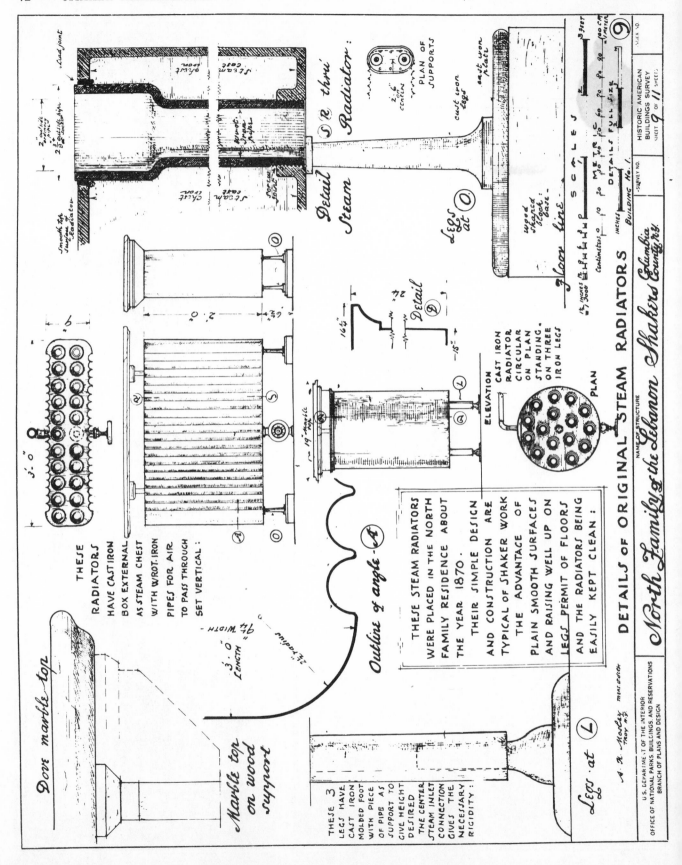

DETAILS of ORIGINAL STEAM RADIATORS

North Family of the Lebanon Shakers Columbia County, N.Y.

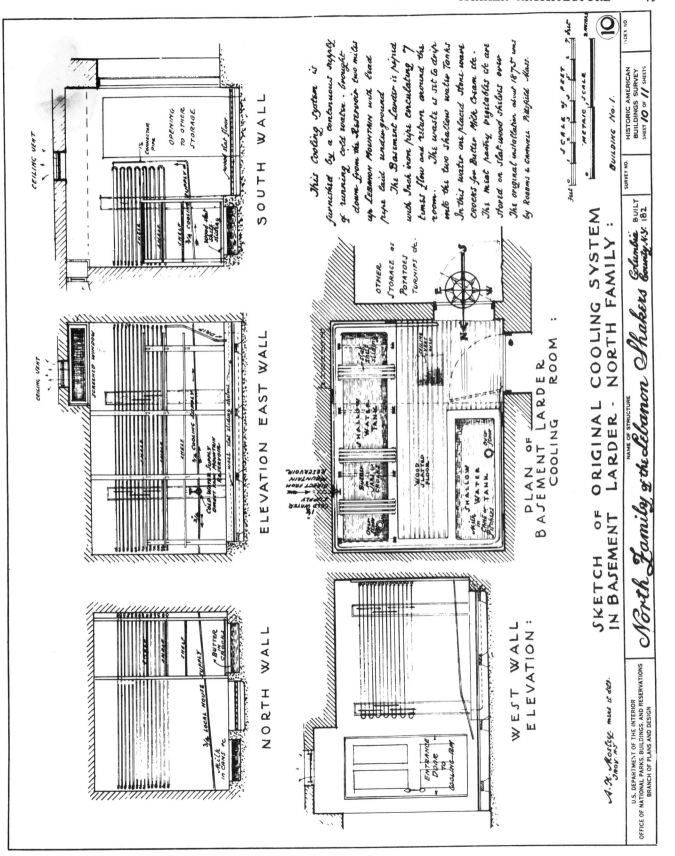

CEILING VENT

½ CONNECTING PIPE

OPENING TO OTHER STORAGE

¾ COOLING SUPPLY

SHELF

SHELF

WOOD SLAT SLIDE FLOOR

Wood slat floor

SOUTH WALL

This Cooling System is furnished by a continuous supply of running cold water, brought down from the Reservoir two miles up Lebanon Mountain with lead pipe laid underground.

The Basement Larder is piped with 1 inch iron pipe circulating 7 times & flow and return around the room. The waste is set to drip into the two shallow water Tanks.

In this water are placed stone ware crocks for Butter Milk Cream &c. This meat poultry vegetables &c are stored on slat wood shelves over.

The original installation about 1873 was by Robbins & Grinnell, Pittsfield Mass.

CEILING VENT

CEILING VENT

SCREENED WINDOW

DRIP

SHELF

SHELF

¾ COOLING SUPPLY

WALL SLAT SLIDING SHELVES

COLD WATER SUPPLY DIRECT FROM MOUNTAIN RESERVOIR

¾

ELEVATION EAST WALL

OTHER STORAGE of POTATOES TURNIPS &c

WALL SLAT SLIDING

DIRECT FROM MOUNTAIN RESERVOIR

SHALLOW WATER TANK

BUTTER in CROCKS

WOOD SLATTED FLOOR

COLD WATER SUPPLY

1" COLD WATER SUPPLY

SHALLOW WATER TANK

MILK in CANS or FILLED

OVER FLOW

E

N

S

W

PLAN of BASEMENT LARDER COOLING ROOM :

SHELF

SHELF

SUPPLY

¾ LOCAL HOUSE

BUTTER in CROCKS

MILK in CANS &c

NORTH WALL

ENTRANCE DOOR TO COOLING BAY

WEST WALL ELEVATION :

A. K. Morse, Mead it del. Troy N.Y.

U.S. DEPARTMENT OF THE INTERIOR
OFFICE OF NATIONAL PARKS, BUILDINGS, AND RESERVATIONS
BRANCH OF PLANS AND DESIGN

SKETCH of ORIGINAL COOLING SYSTEM IN BASEMENT LARDER - NORTH FAMILY :

NAME OF STRUCTURE
North Family of the Lebanon Shakers Columbia County, N.Y.

BUILT 182

SURVEY NO.

HISTORIC AMERICAN BUILDINGS SURVEY
SHEET 10 OF 11 SHEETS

BUILDING No. 1.

SCALE ¼ FEET
METRIC SCALE

INDEX NO.
10

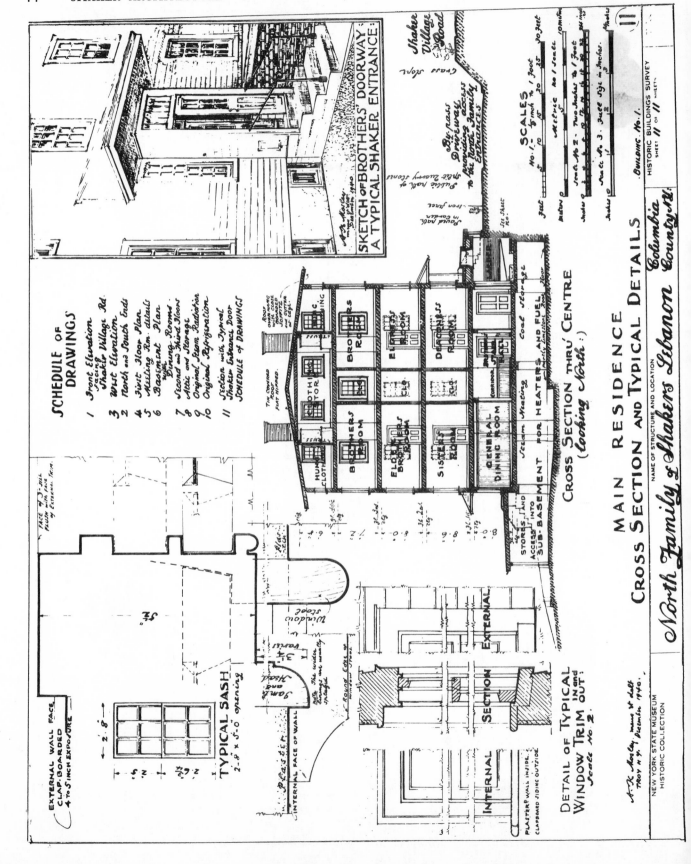

SKETCH OF BROTHERS' DOORWAY:
A TYPICAL SHAKER ENTRANCE:

SCHEDULE OF DRAWINGS

1 Front Elevation facing Shaker Village Rd.
2 North and South Ends
3 West Elevation
4 First Floor Plan
5 Meeting Rm. details
6 Basement Plan
7 Dining Room Second and Third Floor
8 Attic and Storage
9 Original Room Radiation
10 Original Refrigeration
11 Section with Typical Shaker Entrance Door
   SCHEDULE OF DRAWINGS

SCALES

CROSS SECTION thru' CENTRE
(looking North)

EXTERNAL WALL FACE
CLAPBOARDED
4 to 5 inch EXPOSURE

TYPICAL SASH
2'-8" x 5'-0" opening

Window Stool

INTERNAL   SECTION   EXTERNAL

DETAIL OF TYPICAL
WINDOW TRIM IN and OUT:
Scale No. 2.

MAIN RESIDENCE
CROSS SECTION and TYPICAL DETAILS

North Family of Shakers Lebanon Columbia County N.Y.

NEW YORK STATE MUSEUM
HISTORIC COLLECTION

HISTORIC BUILDINGS SURVEY
SHEET 11 OF 11 SHEETS

LAUNDRY BUILDING: NORTH FAMILY, MOUNT LEBANON, NEW YORK

The exterior of this building, as with all other Shaker buildings, is plain and unadorned. The plastered cavetto coves, not uncommon to Shaker buildings, were designed to cut down the escape of heat through the attic during the winter months.

The basement of this building is on the ground level at the west elevation. On the south end is the laundry room; it was well equipped with washing machines, stone washtubs, draining trays, and arch kettles for heating water and scalding laundry.

On the first floor, east entrance, is the large ironing room with sliding clothes racks that were shoved into a special heated compartment for drying laundry during winter months. On the north end are the woodshed and tool repair rooms.

Laundry Building

On the second floor, special rooms were assigned to the seed industry, for storage, and carpet-weaving.

In one of the rooms on the second floor, west side, are the perforated zinc pans for drying fruits and vegetables. These "dry kilns" are installed over hot air conduits which branch off the jacket around the furnace in the basement.

The attic was used for drying seeds, herbs, and the laundry, during the winter months. This building was erected in 1854.

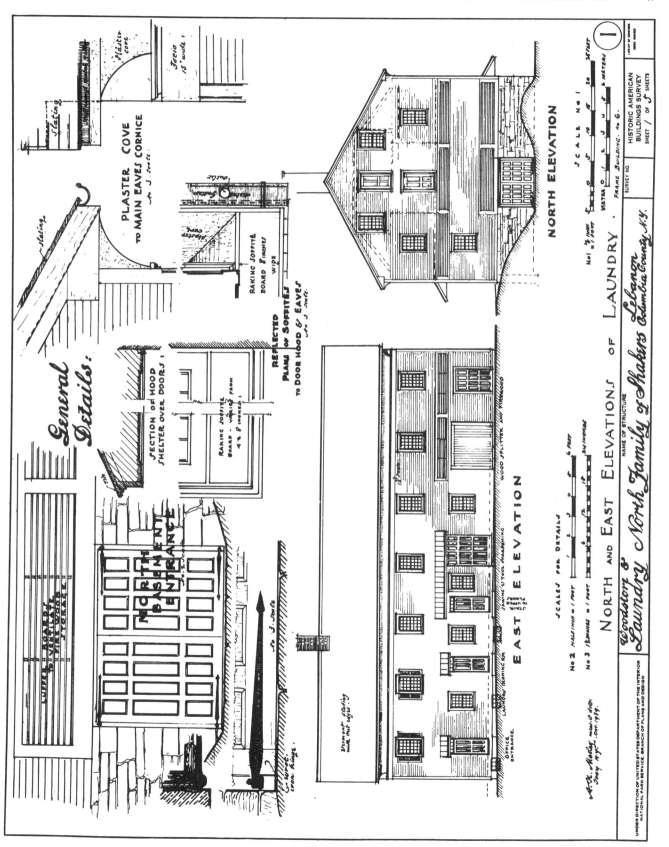

General Details.

PLASTER COVE to MAIN EAVES CORNICE

SECTION of HOOD SHELTER over DOORS.

REFLECTED PLANS or SOFFITS to DOOR HOOD & EAVES

NORTH BASEMENT ENTRANCE

NORTH ELEVATION

EAST ELEVATION

NORTH and EAST ELEVATIONS of LAUNDRY

Woodstore & Laundry of North Family of Shakers Lebanon Columbia County N.Y.

HISTORIC AMERICAN BUILDINGS SURVEY

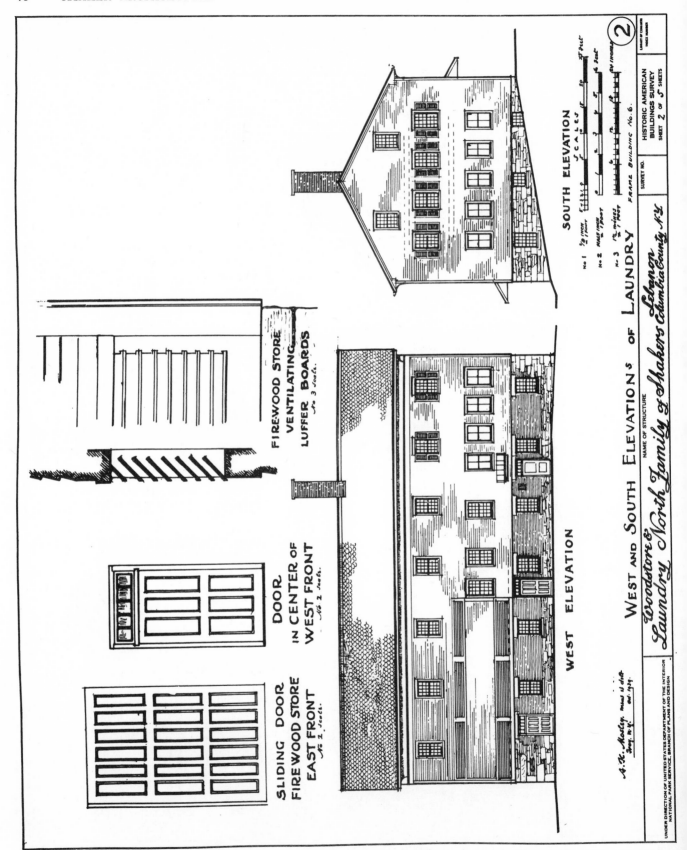

SOUTH ELEVATION

WEST ELEVATION

WEST AND SOUTH ELEVATIONS OF LAUNDRY

FIREWOOD STORE VENTILATING LUFFER BOARDS
No 3 Scale.

DOOR IN CENTER OF WEST FRONT
No 2 Scale.

SLIDING DOOR FIREWOOD STORE EAST FRONT
No 1 Scale.

SCALE
No 1 ½ inch 1 foot
No 2 half inch 1 foot
No 3 ¾ inch 1 foot

SURVEY NO.   HISTORIC AMERICAN BUILDINGS SURVEY
FRAME BUILDING No. 6.   SHEET 2 OF 5 SHEETS

NAME OF STRUCTURE
Woodstore & Laundry of North Family of Shakers Lebanon Columbia County N.Y.

A. K. Motley. Meas'd & dltd. Oct 1939.
Troy, N.Y.

UNDER DIRECTION OF UNITED STATES DEPARTMENT OF THE INTERIOR
NATIONAL PARK SERVICE, BRANCH OF PLANS AND DESIGN

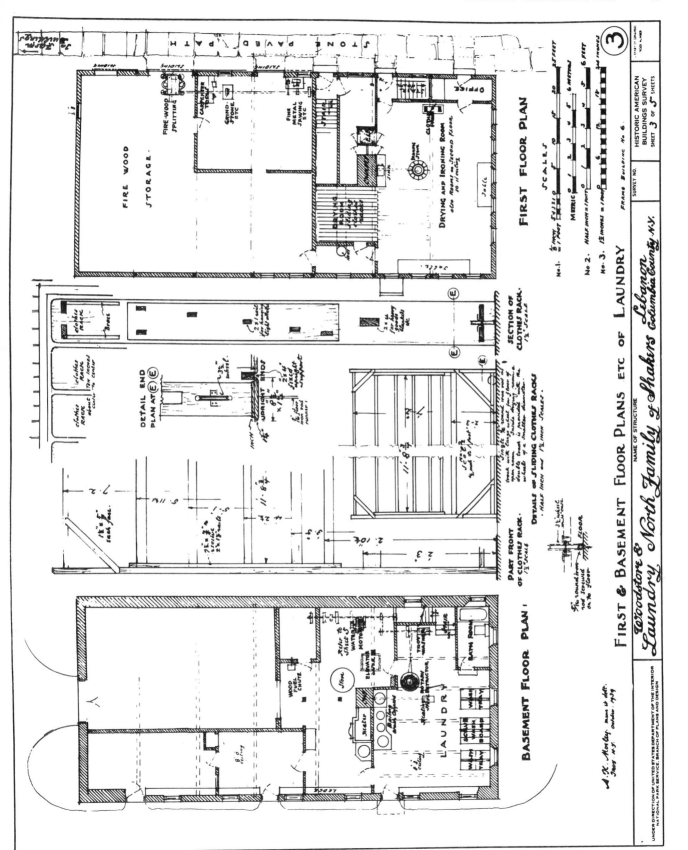

FIRST & BASEMENT FLOOR PLANS etc of LAUNDRY

Woodstore & North Family of Shakers Lebanon
Laundry Columbia County, N.Y.

HISTORIC AMERICAN
BUILDINGS SURVEY
SHEET 3 OF 5 SHEETS

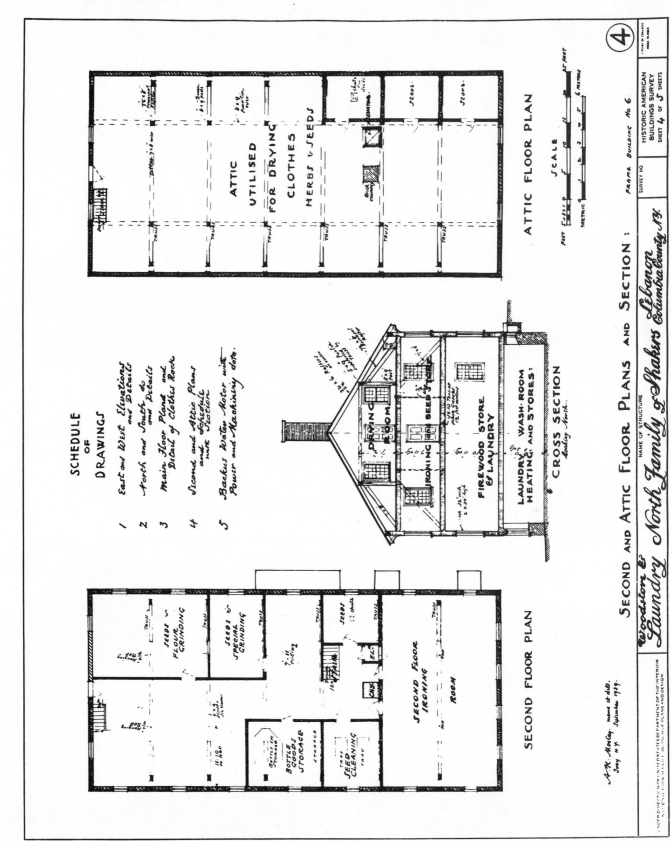

ATTIC FLOOR PLAN

ATTIC UTILISED FOR DRYING CLOTHES HERBS & SEEDS

SCALE

CROSS SECTION
looking South

DINING ROOM

IRONING AND SEED STORE

FIREWOOD STORE & LAUNDRY

LAUNDRY WASH-ROOM HEATING AND STORES

SECOND FLOOR PLAN

SEEDS & FLOUR GRINDING

SEEDS & SPECIAL GRINDING

SEEDS

SECOND FLOOR IRONING ROOM

BOTTLES GOODS STORAGE

TRAY SEED CLEANING

SCHEDULE OF DRAWINGS

1. East and West Elevations and Details
2. North and South do and Details
3. Main Floor Plan and Detail of Clothes Rack
4. Second and Attic Plans and Schedule with Section
5. Backus Water Motor with Power and Machinery data.

SECOND AND ATTIC FLOOR PLANS AND SECTION:

Woodstore & Laundry North Family of Shakers Lebanon Columbia County, N.Y.

NAME OF STRUCTURE

SURVEY NO.   HISTORIC AMERICAN BUILDINGS SURVEY

FRAME BUILDING No 6   SHEET 4 OF 5 SHEETS

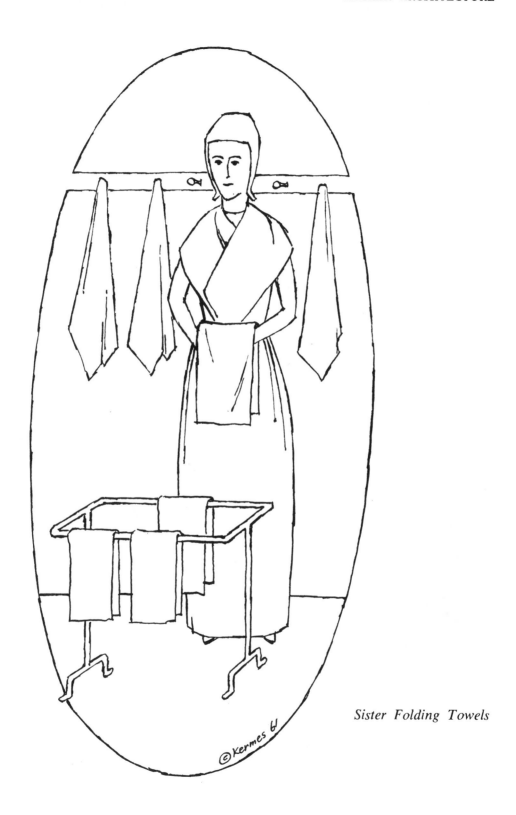

Sister Folding Towels

LUMBER AND GRIST MILL: NORTH FAMILY, MOUNT LEBANON, NEW YORK

The Mount Lebanon mill was erected in 1828. Water from a nearby pond on the Church Family property furnished water power for this mill and the "brethren's brick shop."

This building was demolished in September 1940.

Lumber and Grist Mill

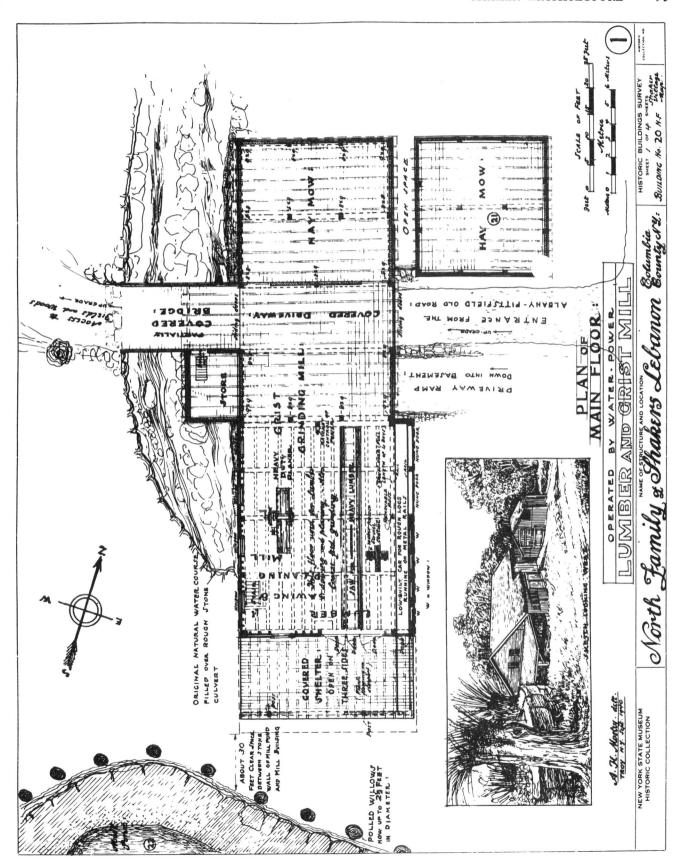

PLAN OF MAIN FLOOR

OPERATED BY WATER-POWER

LUMBER AND GRIST MILL

North Family, of Shakers Lebanon Columbia County N.Y.

NAME OF STRUCTURE AND LOCATION

NEW YORK STATE MUSEUM
HISTORIC COLLECTION

HISTORIC BUILDINGS SURVEY
SHEET 1 OF 4 SHEETS
BUILDING No. 20 N.F.

A.H. Morty. del.
TROY N.Y. Dec 1940

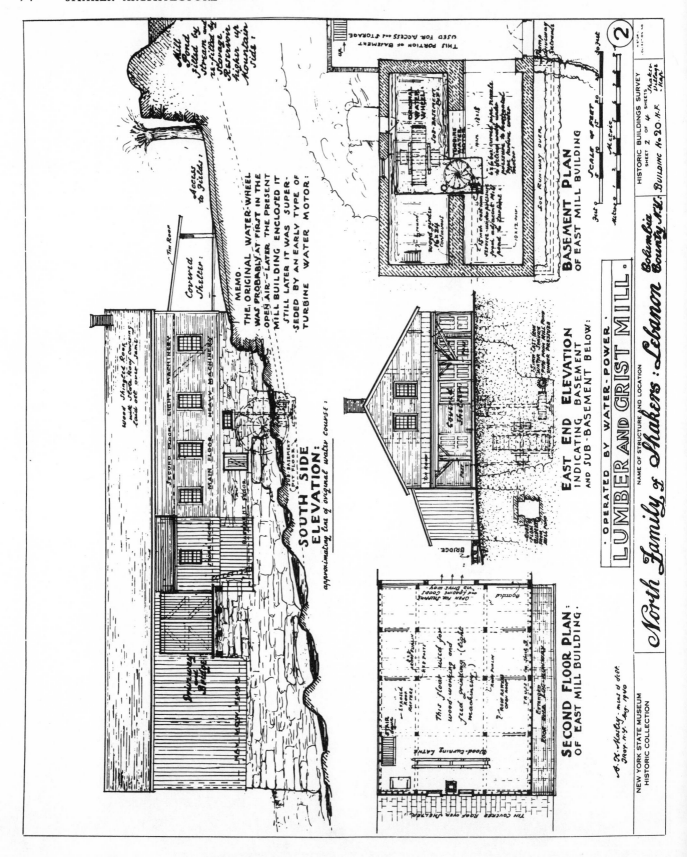

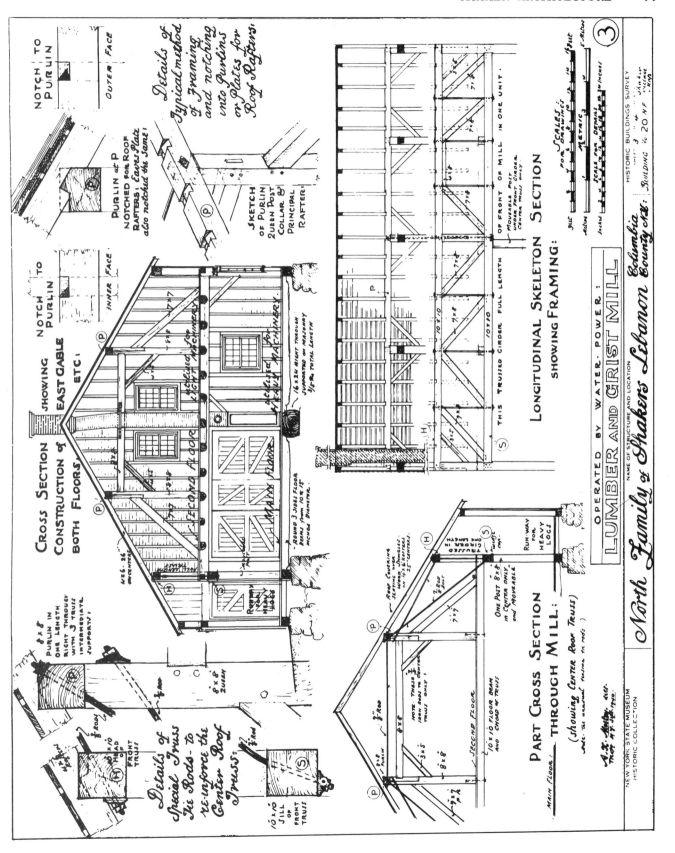

NOTCH TO PURLIN

OUTER FACE

Details of Typical method of framing and notching into Purlins or Plates for Roof Rafters.

PURLIN at P NOTCHED FOR ROOF RAFTERS; EAVES PLATE also notched the Same!

SKETCH OF PURLIN QUEEN POST COLLAR 8" PRINCIPAL RAFTER.

NOTCH PURLIN TO

INNER FACE

CROSS SECTION SHOWING CONSTRUCTION of EAST GABLE AND BOTH FLOORS, ETC!

8 x 8 PURLIN IN ONE LENGTH RIGHT THROUGH WITH 3 TRUSS INTERMEDIATE SUPPORT!

8 x 8 QUEEN

10 x 10 HEAD OF FRONT TRUSS

Details of Special Truss Tie Rods to re-inforce the Center Roof Truss!

10 x 10 SILL OF FRONT TRUSS

THIS TRUSSED GIRDER, FULL LENGTH OF FRONT OF MILL IN ONE UNIT.

LONGITUDINAL SKELETON SECTION SHOWING FRAMING:

PART CROSS SECTION THROUGH MILL: (SHOWING CENTER ROOF TRUSS)

MAIN FLOOR:

SECOND FLOOR

10 x 10 FLOOR BEAM and CHORD OF TRUSS

RUN-WAY FOR HEAVY LOGS

TRUSSED GIRDER IN ONE LENGTH

One Post 8 x 8 IN CENTER ONLY and MOVABLE

ROOF COVERING

SCALES:
FOR DRAWING
METRIC
SCALE FOR DETAILS

OPERATED BY WATER POWER:

NAME OF STRUCTURE AND LOCATION

North Family of Shakers Lebanon Columbia County N.Y.

LUMBER AND GRIST MILL

HISTORIC BUILDINGS SURVEY
BUILDING No. 20 N.F.

A. K. Author, del.

NEW YORK STATE MUSEUM
HISTORIC COLLECTION

3

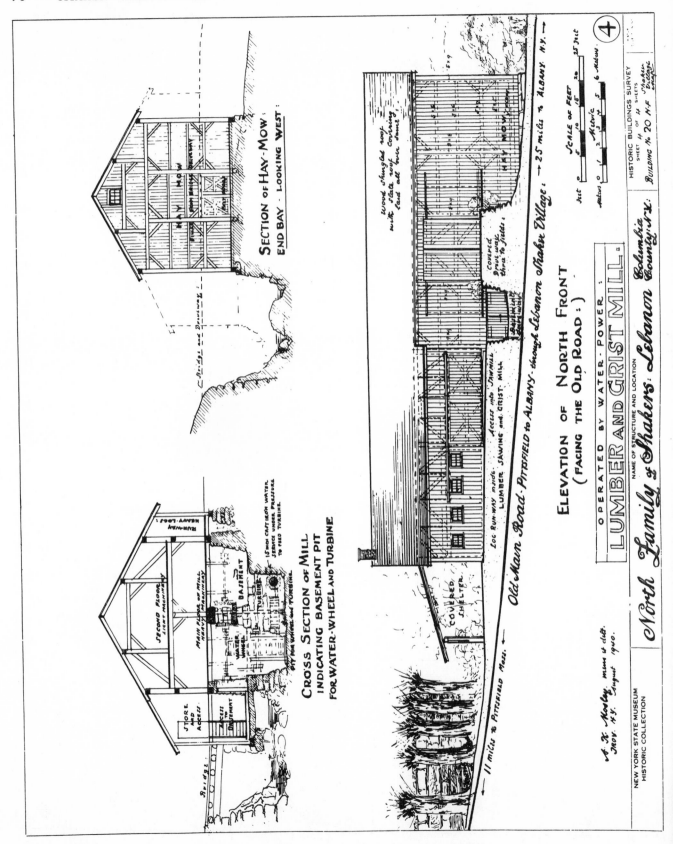

SECTION of HAY·MOW·
END BAY · LOOKING WEST :

CROSS SECTION of MILL
INDICATING BASEMENT PIT
FOR WATER·WHEEL AND TURBINE

ELEVATION of NORTH FRONT
(FACING THE OLD ROAD :)

OPERATED BY WATER·POWER·

LUMBER AND GRIST MILL·

North Family of Shakers: Lebanon Columbia County N.Y.

NEW YORK STATE MUSEUM
HISTORIC COLLECTION

NAME OF STRUCTURE AND LOCATION

HISTORIC BUILDINGS SURVEY
SHEET 4 of 14 SHEETS
BUILDING No 20 N·F   Shaker Village

A Shaker Carpenter

BRETHREN'S RED BRICK SHOP: NORTH FAMILY, MOUNT LEBANON, NEW YORK

A three-story red brick building, with attic and basement, was erected in 1825. Windows were formed of flat gauged brick arches and sills of sawed Stockbridge marble. The basement walls are made of the same sawed marble.

Originally this was the laundry building, but in later years it was known as the "Brethren's Red Brick Shop." This building accommodated the shoemaker's shop, the broom shop, carpenters' shops, and seed shops.

Brethren's Red Brick Shop

The large power wheel in the basement was propelled by water from the same stream that turned the lumber and grist mill power wheels.

According to the Millennial Law, Sev. V, Art 23: "Brethren's and sisters' shops should not be under one and the same roof, except those of the Ministry."

In the Shoemaker's Shop

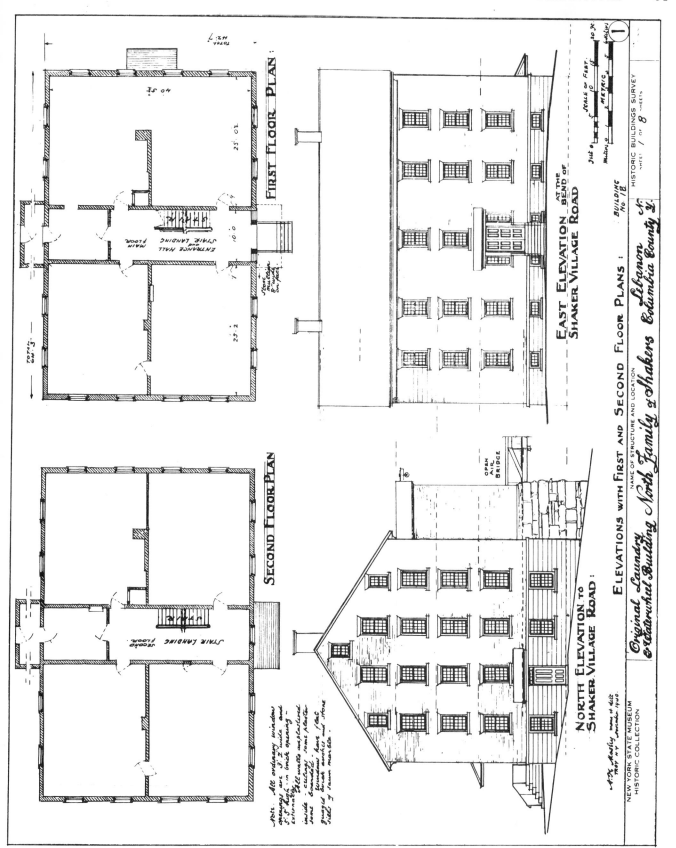

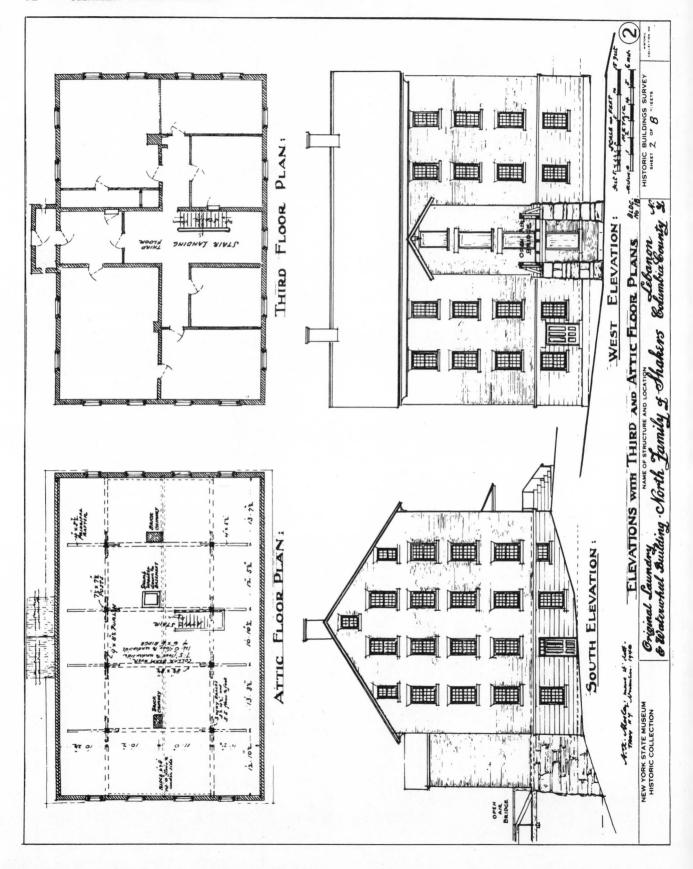

THIRD FLOOR PLAN:

STAIR LANDING

THIRD FLOOR

ATTIC FLOOR PLAN:

WEST ELEVATION:

SOUTH ELEVATION:

OPEN AIR BRIDGE

ELEVATIONS WITH THIRD AND ATTIC FLOOR PLANS

Original Laundry & Waterwheel Building · North Family of Shakers · Lebanon · Columbia County

NEW YORK STATE MUSEUM
HISTORIC COLLECTION

NAME OF STRUCTURE AND LOCATION

HISTORIC BUILDINGS SURVEY
SHEET 2 OF 8 SHEETS

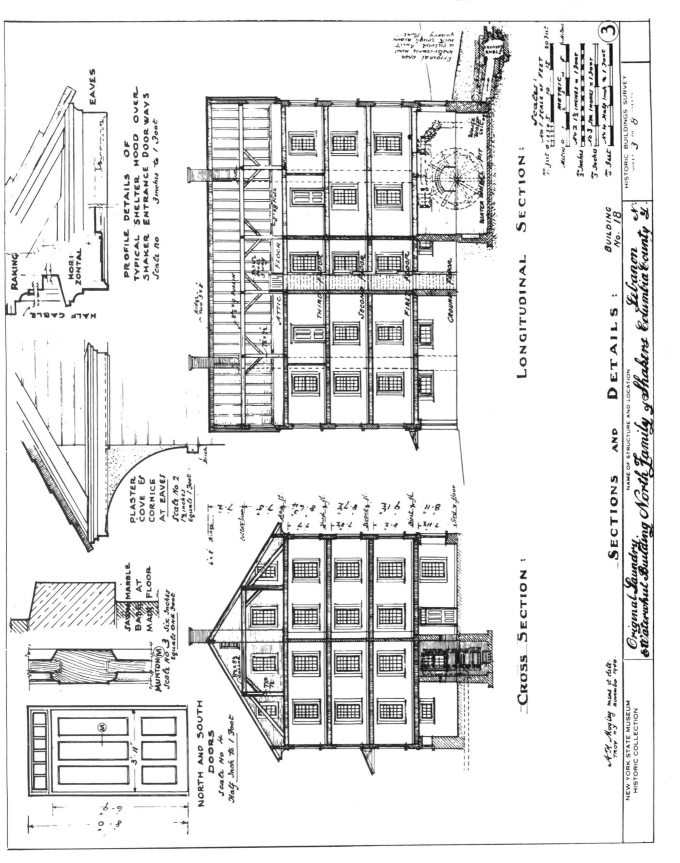

EAVES

RAKING

HORIZONTAL

HALF GABLE

PROFILE DETAILS OF TYPICAL SHELTER HOOD OVER SHAKER ENTRANCE DOOR WAYS
Scale No 3 inches to 1 foot

PLASTER COVE & CORNICE AT EAVES
Scale No 2 1½ inches equals 1 foot

Brick

MARBLE AT FLOOR

SAD BASE MADE

MUNTON (M)
Scale No 3 Six inches equals one foot

NORTH AND SOUTH DOORS
Scale No 4 Half inch to 1 foot

CROSS SECTION:

LONGITUDINAL SECTION:

Scale No 1 Scale of FEET

Metric

HISTORIC BUILDINGS SURVEY
SHEET 3 OF 8

SECTIONS AND DETAILS:
BUILDING No. 18

Original Laundry
& Waterwheel Building North Family of Shakers Columbia County L.
Lebanon N.Y.

A.H. Mosig med it det.
Troy N.Y. November 1940

NEW YORK STATE MUSEUM
HISTORIC COLLECTION

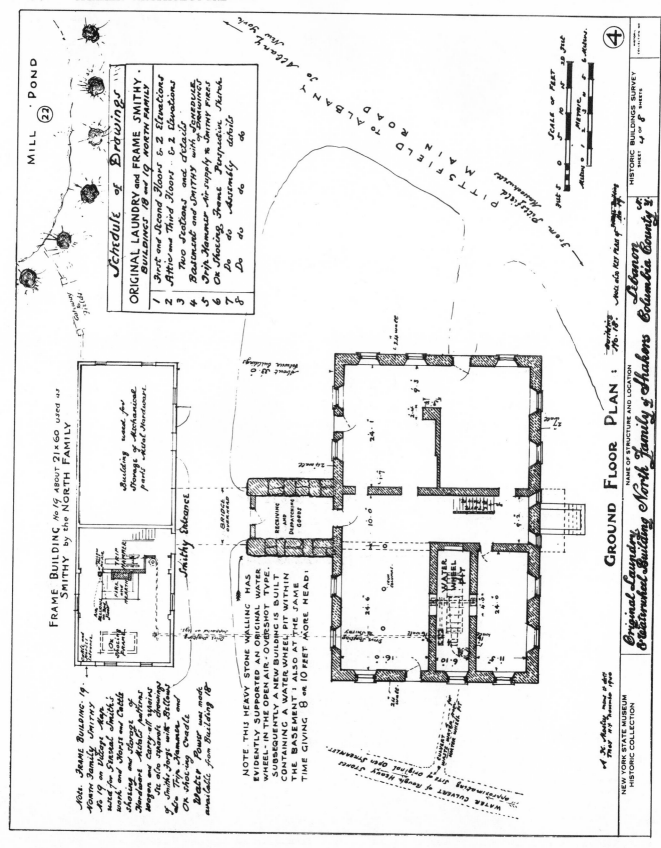

MEETING HOUSE: CHURCH FAMILY, MOUNT LEBANON, NEW YORK

This meeting house was erected in 1824 entirely by the brethren of Lebanon; Watervliet, New York; Enfield, New Hampshire and Shirley, Massachusetts, and other Shaker communities. The total cost was estimated by Brother Alonzo Hollister to have been more than $16,000. Of this amount, the Shakers of Canterbury and Enfield, New Hampshire, contributed $500, and the Societies at Enfield, Connecticut, and Hancock, Massachusetts, donated $600. The Church Family of the Harvard, Massachusetts, Society furnished the glass for the windows. The Shirley, Massachusetts, Society donated the services cf Brother Jonas Nutting from July 12 to September 15, 1824.

Meeting House

This is one of the most interesting buildings to be found in any Shaker community. The barrel, or rainbow roof, planned to shed snow, and its intricate supporting frame work are worthy of special study. The Meeting Room, sixty-three feet by seventy-eight feet four inches, has no interior suuports. The two chimneys (north and south walls) were designed for the four large cast-iron stoves that heated the auditorium or "Meeting Room." These stoves are now in the Shaker Museum, Old Chatham, New York.

The wing on the south side housed members of the Ministry, elders, and eldresses. It provided work rooms as well as retiring rooms for them.

The entrance doorway to this wing embodies another beautiful architectural detail in Shaker buildings, but certainly unintentional, because the Millennial Laws constantly forbade planned beauty. The combination of rightness of line and proportion achieved a work of art in this detail.

"The Meeting House should be painted white without and of a bluish shade within. . . . No building may be white save meeting houses." Millennial Law, Sec. I, Arts. 3 and 6.

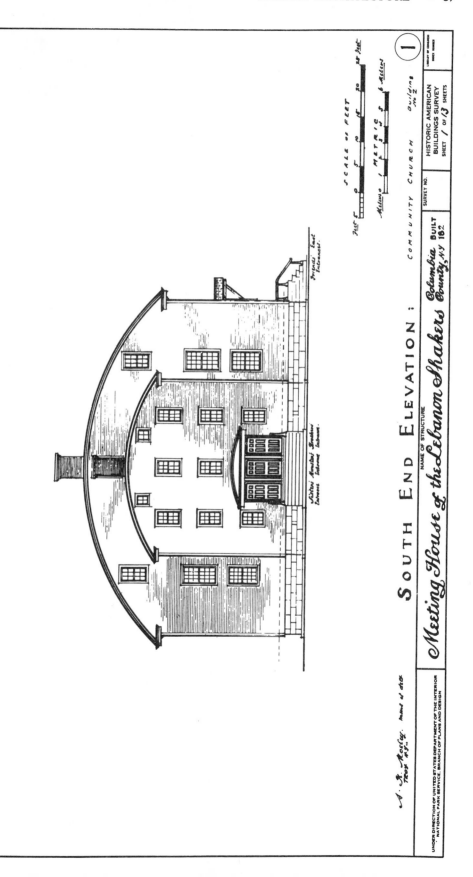

SOUTH END ELEVATION: COMMUNITY CHURCH

Meeting House of the Lebanon Shakers Columbia County, N.Y. BUILT 182

SCALE of FEET

METRIC'S

Pictorial East Entrance

Central Arched Meadows Entrance

HISTORIC AMERICAN BUILDINGS SURVEY
SHEET 1 OF 13 SHEETS

UNDER DIRECTION OF UNITED STATES DEPARTMENT OF THE INTERIOR
NATIONAL PARK SERVICE, BRANCH OF PLANS AND DESIGN

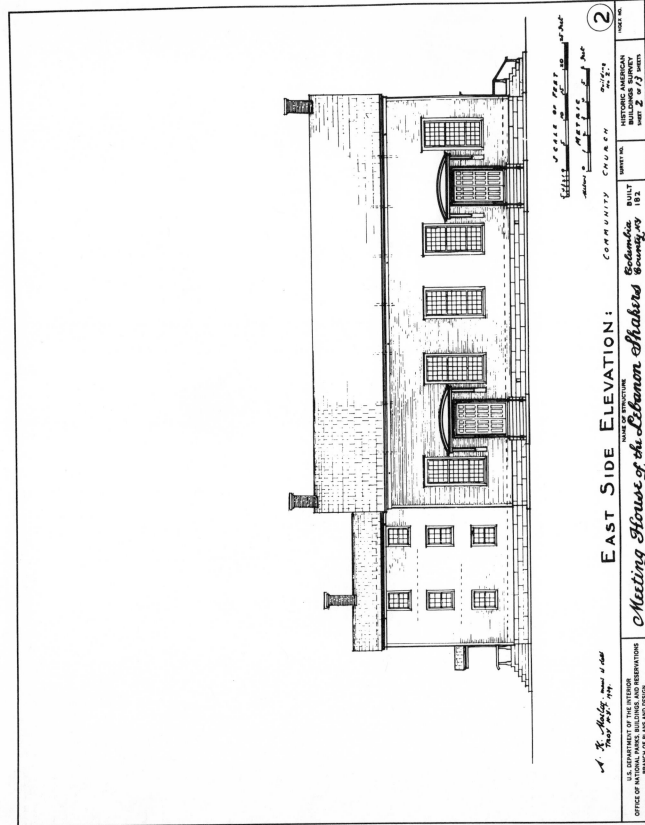

EAST SIDE ELEVATION: COMMUNITY CHURCH

Meeting House of the Lebanon Shakers Columbia County, N.Y.

NAME OF STRUCTURE

BUILT 182

SURVEY NO.

HISTORIC AMERICAN BUILDINGS SURVEY
SHEET 2 OF 13 SHEETS

INDEX NO. 2

SCALE OF FEET

METRIC

Drawing no 2:

U.S. DEPARTMENT OF THE INTERIOR
OFFICE OF NATIONAL PARKS, BUILDINGS, AND RESERVATIONS
BRANCH OF PLANS AND DESIGN

A. K. Holley, Troy N.Y. 1949.

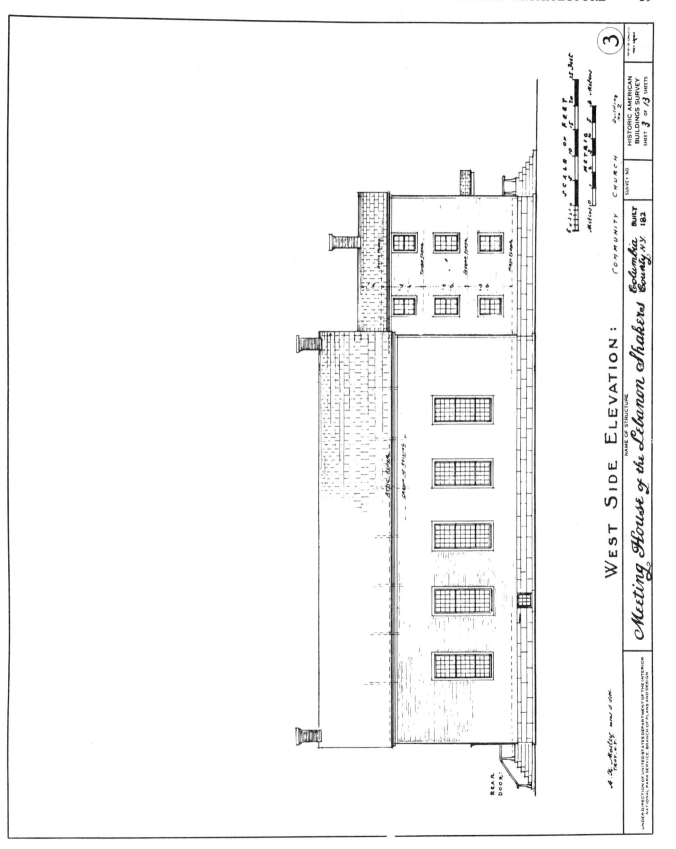

WEST SIDE ELEVATION:

Meeting House of the Lebanon Shakers

REAR DOOR:

ATTIC FLOOR

LEDGE OF EAVES

ATTIC FLOOR

THIRD FLOOR

SECOND FLOOR

MAIN FLOOR

A. R. Marley draftsman
Troy, N.Y.

UNDER DIRECTION OF UNITED STATES DEPARTMENT OF THE INTERIOR
NATIONAL PARK SERVICE BRANCH OF PLANS AND DESIGN

NAME OF STRUCTURE

COMMUNITY CHURCH

Columbia County, N.Y.

BUILT 182

SURVEY NO.

Building No. 2

HISTORIC AMERICAN
BUILDINGS SURVEY
SHEET 3 OF 13 SHEETS

3

SCALE OF FEET

METRIC

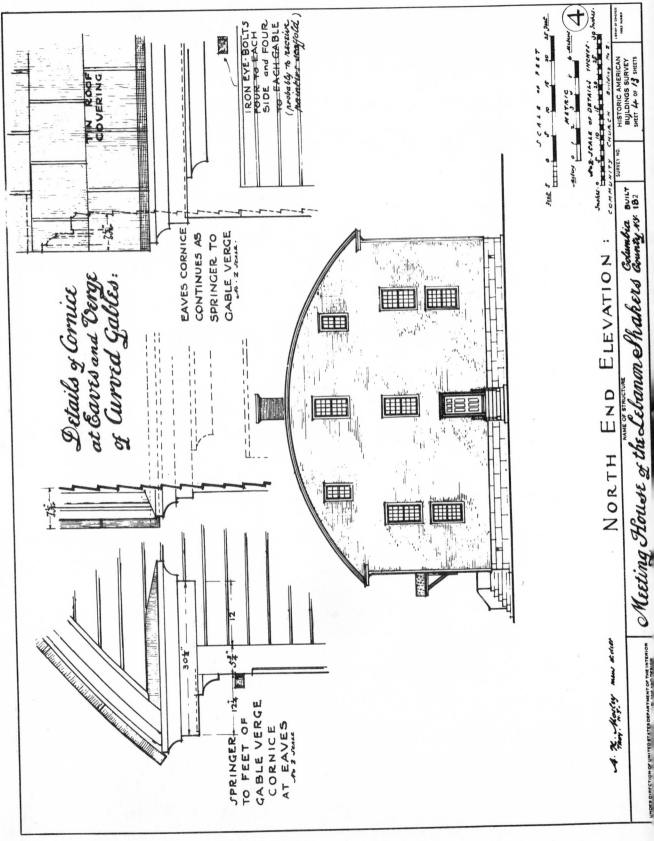

TIN ROOF COVERING

Details of Cornice at Eaves and Verge of Curved Gables:

EAVES CORNICE CONTINUES AS SPRINGER TO GABLE VERGE
No 2 Scale

IRON EYE-BOLTS FOUR TO EACH SIDE and FOUR TO EACH GABLE
(probably to receive painters' scaffold)

SPRINGER TO FEET OF GABLE VERGE CORNICE AT EAVES
No 2 Scale

30"

12¼

12

3¼"

A. R. Healy new artist
Troy, N.Y.

NORTH END ELEVATION:

Meeting House of the Lebanon Shakers Columbia County N.Y.

SCALE OF FEET

METRIC

½" SCALE OF DETAILS INCHES

COMMUNITY NO.

NAME OF STRUCTURE

SURVEY NO.

HISTORIC AMERICAN BUILDINGS SURVEY

SHEET 4 of 13 SHEETS

BUILT 1B2

CHURCH Building No. 2

4

UNDER DIRECTION OF UNITED STATES DEPARTMENT OF THE INTERIOR
R. AND AND DESIGN

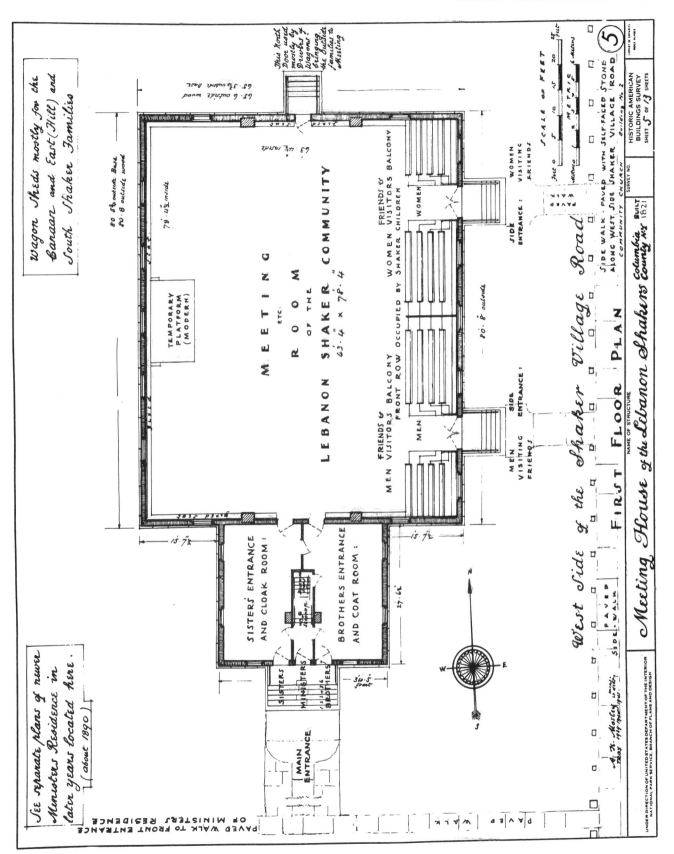

Meeting House of the Lebanon Shakers

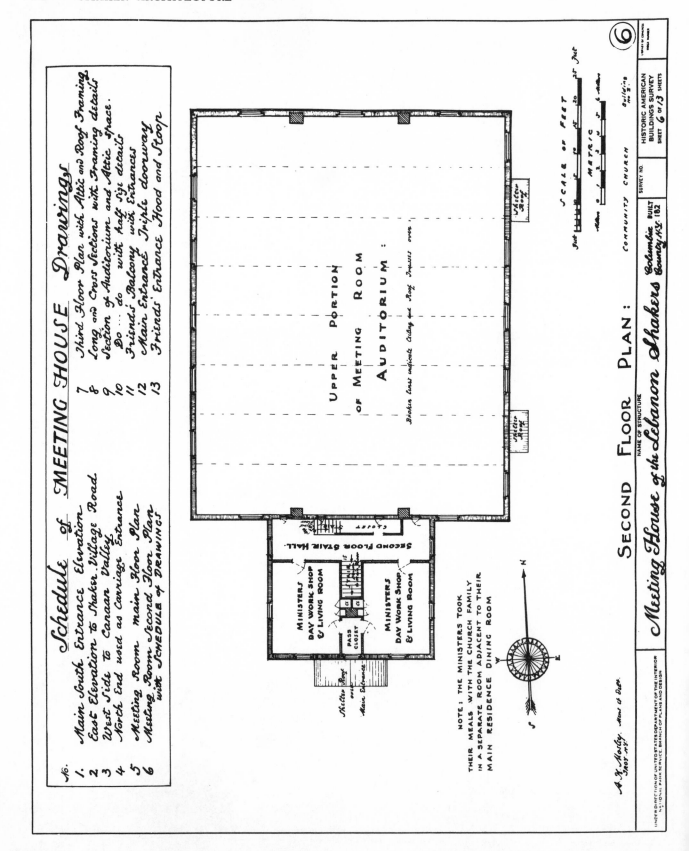

Schedule of MEETING HOUSE Drawings

No.
1. Main South Entrance Elevation
2. East Elevation to Shaker Village Road
3. West Side to Canaan Valley
4. North End used as Carriage Entrance
5. Meeting Room main Floor Plan
6. Meeting Room Second Floor Plan with SCHEDULE of DRAWINGS

7. Third Floor Plan with Attic and Roof Framing
8. Long and Cross Sections with framing details
9. Section of Auditorium and Attic space
10. Do.....do....with half size details
11. Friends Balcony with Entrance
12. Main Entrance Triple doorway
13. Friends Entrance Hood and Stoop

UPPER PORTION of MEETING ROOM AUDITORIUM:

SECOND FLOOR PLAN: Meeting House of the Lebanon Shakers

NOTE: THE MINISTERS TOOK THEIR MEALS WITH THE CHURCH FAMILY IN A SEPARATE ROOM ADJACENT TO THEIR MAIN RESIDENCE DINING ROOM

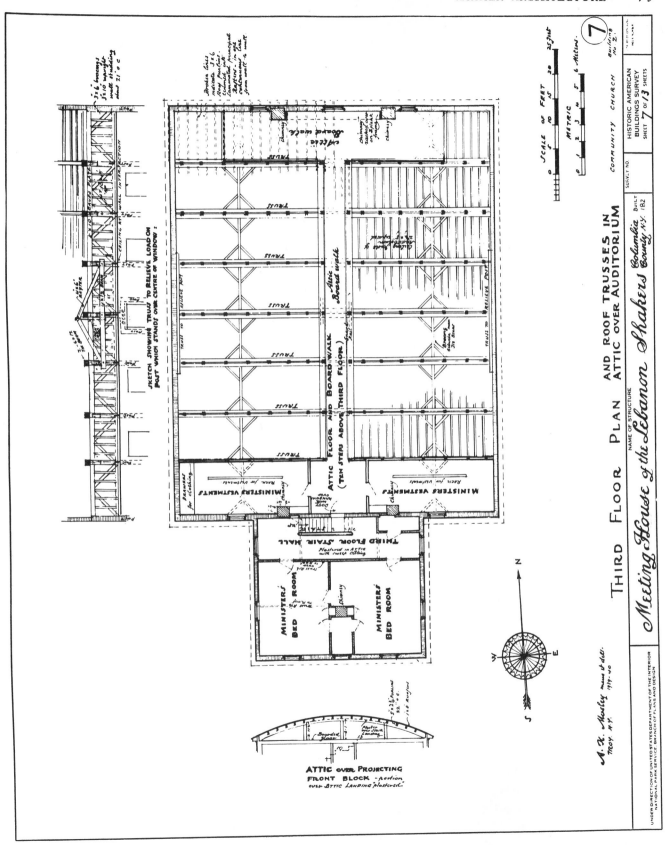

THIRD FLOOR PLAN AND ROOF TRUSSES IN ATTIC OVER AUDITORIUM

Meeting House of the Lebanon Shakers Columbia County N.Y.

ATTIC OVER PROJECTING FRONT BLOCK -portion over Attic Landing plastered.

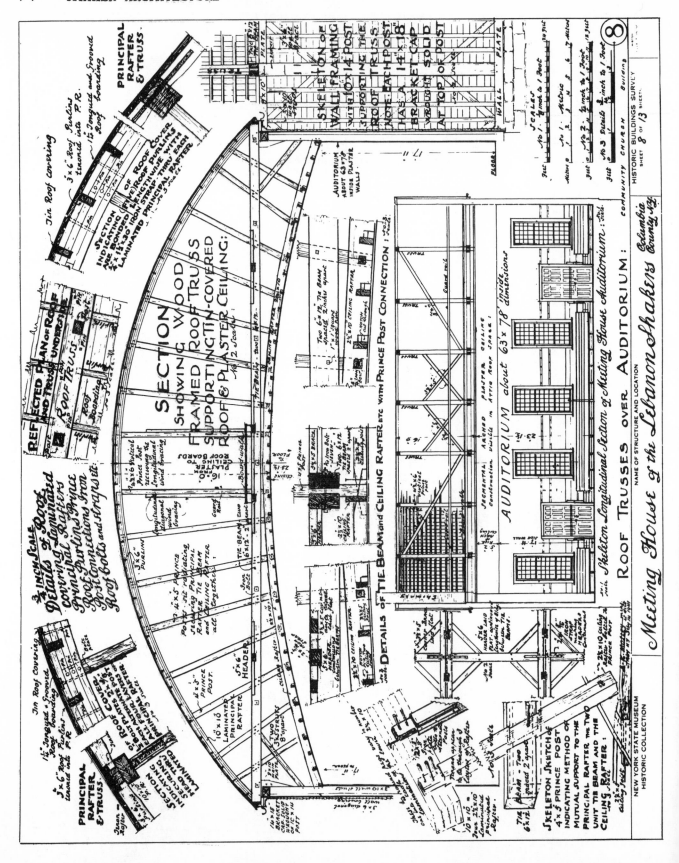

PRINCIPAL RAFTER & TRUSS.

Tin Roof covering

3 x 6 Roof Purlins tenoned into P.R.

1¼ Tongued and Grooved Roof boarding

SECTION INDICATING THAT ROOF COVERING ARE BONDED TO ROOF PURLINS. WEIR ROOF LENGTHWISE WITH 4 x 12 x 30 IRON STRAP. THRU EACH LAMINATED PRINCIPAL RAFTER.

SKELETON OF WALL FRAMING WITH 10 x 14 POST SUPPORTING THE ROOF TRUSS. NOTE EACH POST HAS A 14 x 18 BRACKET CAP WROUGHT SOLID AT TOP OF POST.

TRUSS

9 x 10

WALL PLATE

AUDITORIUM ABOUT 63 x 78 INSIDE PLASTER WALLS

17"

FLOOR

SECTION SHOWING WOOD FRAMED ROOF TRUSS SUPPORTING TIN-COVERED ROOF & PLASTER CEILING.

REFLECTED PLAN OF ROOF AND TRUSS UNDERSIDE

ROOF TRUSS

Roof Boarding

3 INCH SCALE
Details of Roof covering laminated Principal Rafters covering Purlins Prince Post Connections from Roof Bolts and straps etc.

PRINCIPAL RAFTER & TRUSS

Tin Roof covering

1¼ Tongued & Grooved Roof boarding

3 x 6 Roof Purlins tenoned into P.R.

ROOFS COVER 2 x 3 PLANES INVERTED IRON PLANE PIN BEARING 3

SECTION INDICATING SIDE SWAYING

DETAILS OF THE TIE BEAM and CEILING RAFTER etc WITH PRINCE POST CONNECTION

Two 6 x 12 Tie Beam spaced 2 inches apart

3 x 6 CEILING RAFTER

SEGMENTAL ARCHED PLASTER CEILING construction visible in attic roof space

AUDITORIUM about 63 x 78 inside dimensions

Skeleton Longitudinal Section of Meeting House Auditorium

ROOF TRUSSES over AUDITORIUM:

Meeting House of the Lebanon Shakers, Columbia County N.Y.

PRINCE POST

4 x 8 PRINCE POST-

10 x 10 LAMINATED PRINCIPAL RAFTER

6 x 6 HEADER

TIE BEAM 6 x 12

Iron Bolt

Two 3 Struts 8 apart

SKELETON Sketch of 4 x 8 PRINCE POST INDICATING METHOD OF MUTUAL SUPPORT TO THE PRINCIPAL RAFTER the TWO UNIT TIE BEAM and the CEILING RAFTER

NEW YORK STATE MUSEUM HISTORIC COLLECTION

HISTORIC BUILDINGS SURVEY
SHEET 8 of 13

COMMUNITY CHURCH Building

NAME OF STRUCTURE AND LOCATION

No SCALE
No 1. Symbol to 1 Foot
No 2. ½ inch to 1 Foot
No 3. ¼ inch to 1 Foot

8

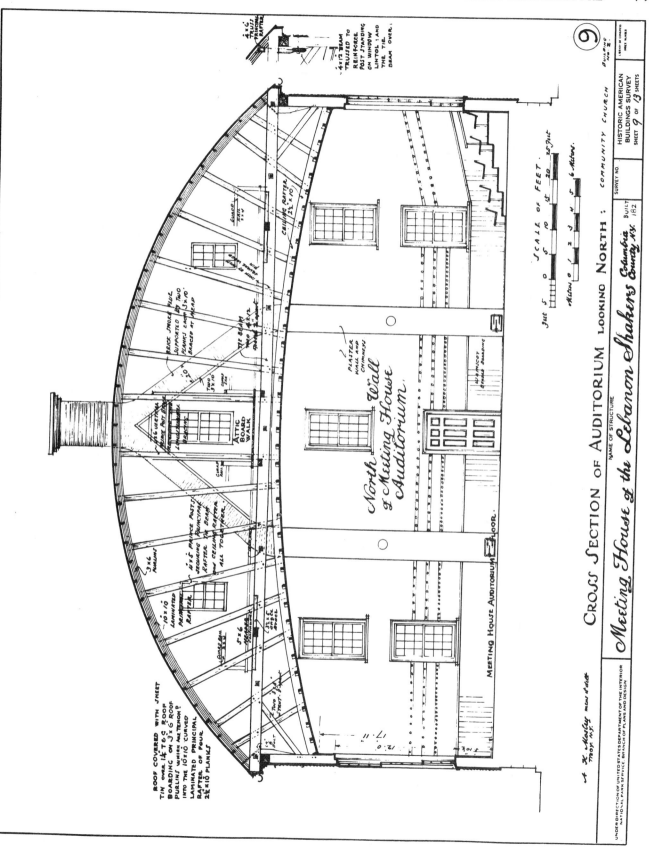

CROSS SECTION OF AUDITORIUM LOOKING NORTH:

Meeting House of the Lebanon Shakers Columbia County, N.Y.

NAME OF STRUCTURE COMMUNITY CHURCH

BUILT 1824

SURVEY NO.

HISTORIC AMERICAN
BUILDINGS SURVEY
SHEET 9 OF 13 SHEETS

UNDER DIRECTION OF UNITED STATES DEPARTMENT OF THE INTERIOR
NATIONAL PARK SERVICE, BRANCH OF PLANS AND DESIGN

A. K. Morley meas d scale
Troy, N.Y.

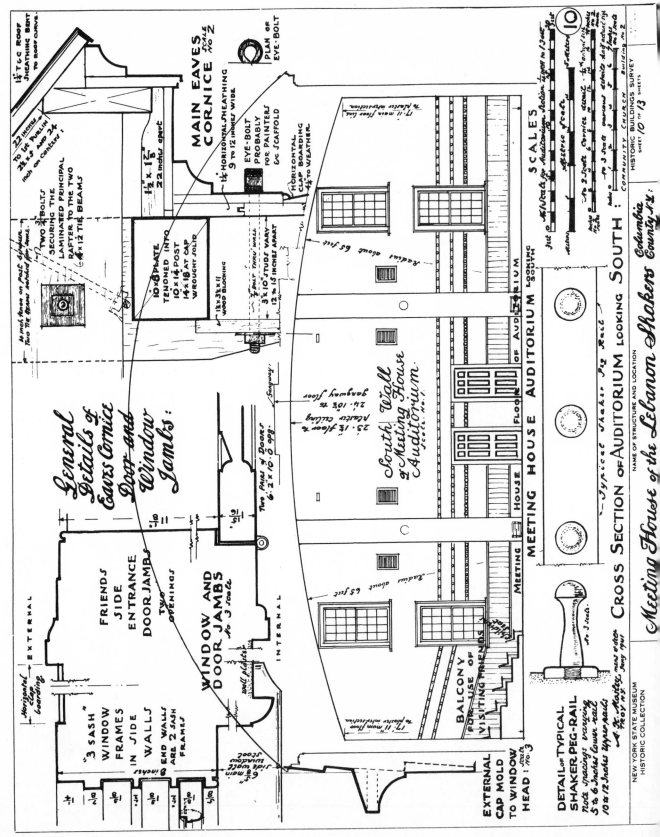

Meeting House of the Lebanon Shakers, Columbia County N.Y.

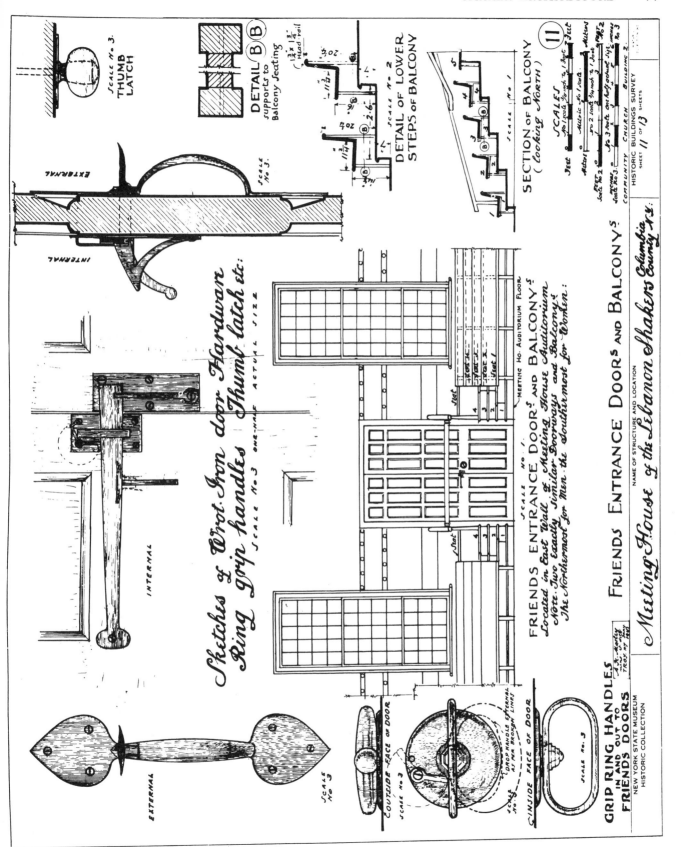

SCALE No. 3.
THUMB
LATCH

DETAIL B B
supports to
Balcony Seating

$\frac{3}{4} \times 1\frac{3}{4}$
Head rail

DETAIL OF LOWER
STEPS of BALCONY

SCALE No. 2

SECTION of BALCONY
(looking North)

11

SCALES

EXTERNAL

INTERNAL

Sketches of Wrot Iron door Hardwar
Ring grip handles & Thumb latch etc:
SCALE No 3   ONE HALF ACTUAL SIZE

INTERNAL

FRIENDS ENTRANCE DOORS and BALCONYS
Located in East Wall of Meeting House Auditorium
Note: Two exactly similar Doorways and Balcony.
The Northermost for Men, the Southermost for Women:

FRIENDS ENTRANCE DOORS and BALCONYS

Meeting House of the Lebanon Shakers Columbia County N.Y.

GRIP RING HANDLES
IN AND OUT TO
FRIENDS DOORS

NEW YORK STATE MUSEUM
HISTORIC COLLECTION

EXTERNAL

SCALE No 3

COUTSIDE FACE of DOOR

INSIDE FACE of DOOR

SCALE No 3

HISTORIC BUILDINGS SURVEY
COMMUNITY CHURCH BUILDING 2.
SHEET 11 OF 13 SHEETS

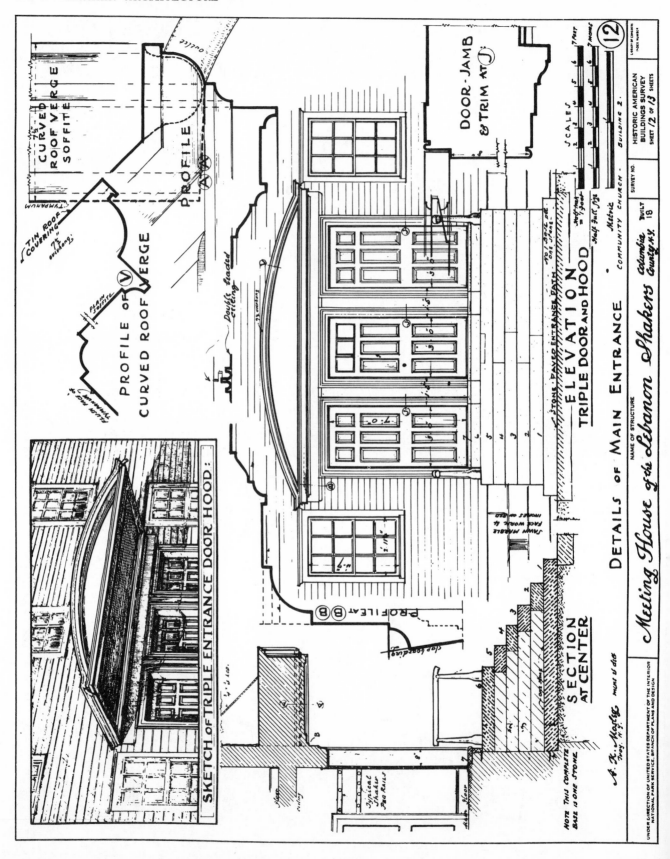

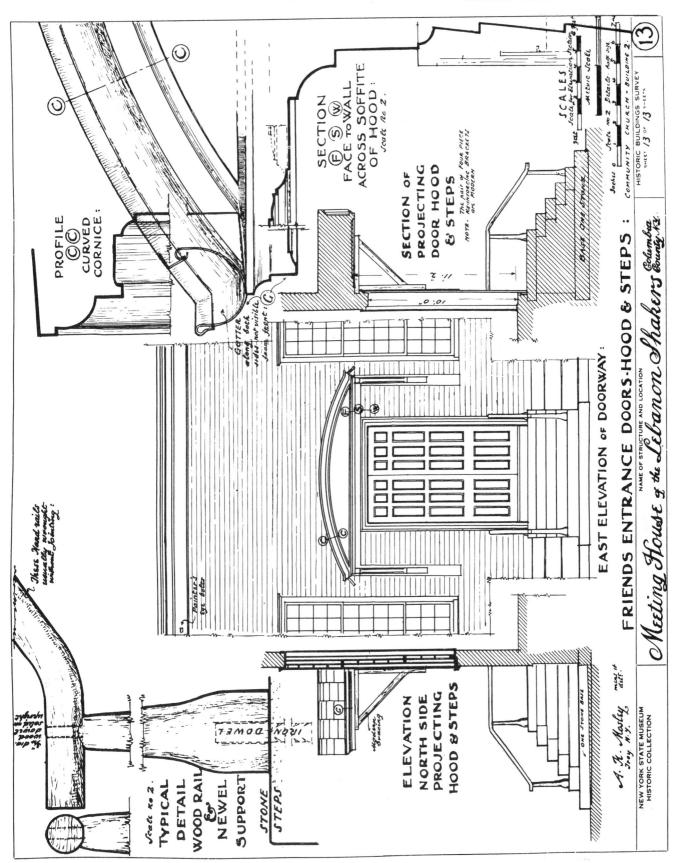

PROFILE C—C CURVED CORNICE:

SECTION F S W FACE to WALL ACROSS SOFFITE OF HOOD: Scale No. 2.

SECTION OF PROJECTING DOOR HOOD & STEPS

The rail is four piece NOTE: Reinforcing Brackets are MODERN.

GUTTER along back side:—not visible from front: C.

Painted tye color

ELEVATION of DOORWAY:

These Hand rails usually wrought without dowel:

TYPICAL DETAIL WOOD RAIL & NEWEL SUPPORT

Scale No. 2.

STONE STEPS

IRON DOWEL

ELEVATION NORTH SIDE PROJECTING HOOD & STEPS

ONE STONE BASE

SCALES

Scale for Elevation Section

Metric Scale

Scale No. 2 Details

Inches

EAST ELEVATION of DOORWAY:

FRIENDS ENTRANCE DOORS · HOOD & STEPS :

NAME OF STRUCTURE AND LOCATION

Meeting House of the Lebanon Shakers Columbia County N.Y.

A. F. Morley, Troy, N.Y.

NEW YORK STATE MUSEUM HISTORIC COLLECTION

HISTORIC BUILDINGS SURVEY
COMMUNITY CHURCH · BUILDING 2.
SHEET 13 of 13 SHEETS

13

An Entrance to the Meeting House

MINISTRY'S DWELLING HOUSE: CHURCH FAMILY, MOUNT LEBANON, NEW YORK

"Odd or fanciful styles of architecture may not be used among the Believers: neither should any deviate widely from the common styles of buildings among Believers, without the Union of the Leaders or Ministry." Millennial Laws, Sec. IX, Art 2.

The above law was broken when this red brick building was erected, for there is a great deviation from the traditional Shaker style of architecture. It has decorative window and door arches, and mouldings and cornices which are far too ornate to pass unnoticed in a Shaker community.

Who was at fault will never be known. Did the Ministry give its consent to these changes, or was it the employed world's laborer who could not

Ministry's Dwelling House

get away from the prevailing Victorian influence? There are, however, many Shaker features embodied such as the off-center front doors, cut stone foundation, and other exterior and interior details.

The building was erected for the use of the Ministry at the time of the construction of the Main Dwelling House in 1875. The stone, dated 1841 and imbedded in the foundation of rear of the wing, is from the first Ministry House, one of the eight buildings destroyed by a pyromaniacal hired man on the evening of February 6, 1875.

Members of the Ministry

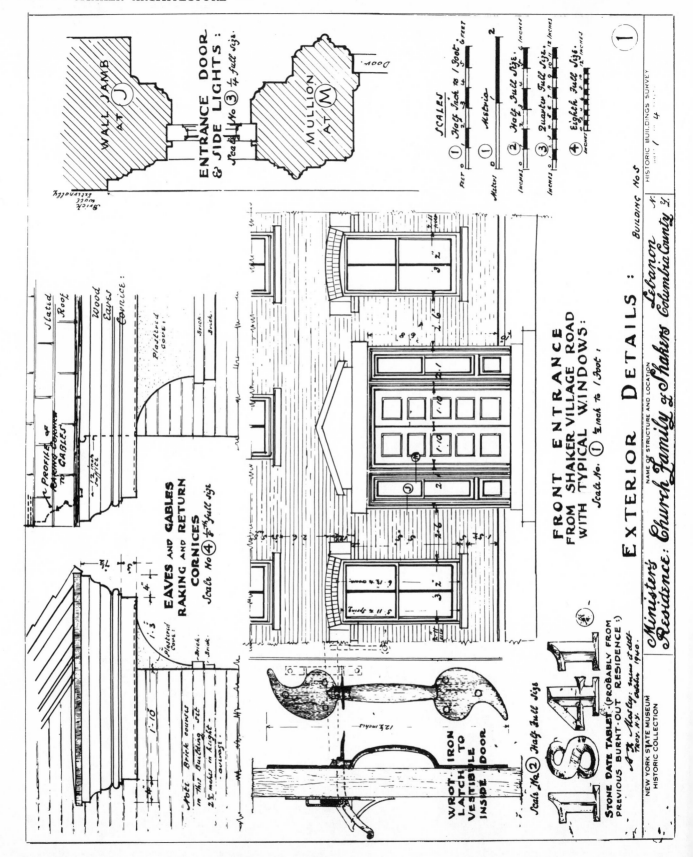

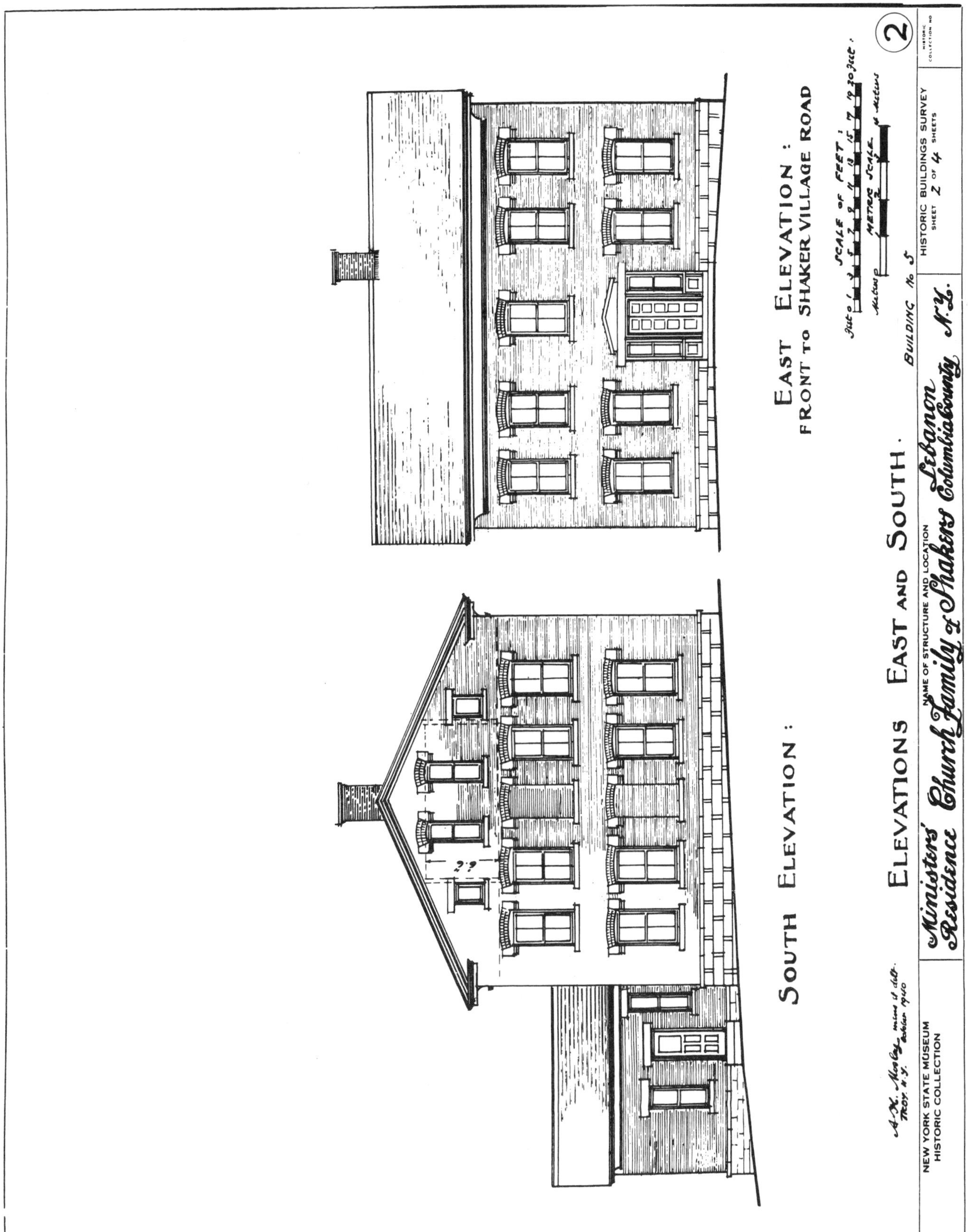

EAST ELEVATION:
FRONT TO SHAKER VILLAGE ROAD

SOUTH ELEVATION:

ELEVATIONS EAST AND SOUTH.

Ministers'
Residence Church Family of Shakers Lebanon Columbia County, N.Y.

BUILDING No 5

SCALE OF FEET

METRIC SCALE

HISTORIC BUILDINGS SURVEY
SHEET 2 OF 4 SHEETS

A.K. Morley measured & delineated
Troy N.Y. October 1940

NEW YORK STATE MUSEUM
HISTORIC COLLECTION

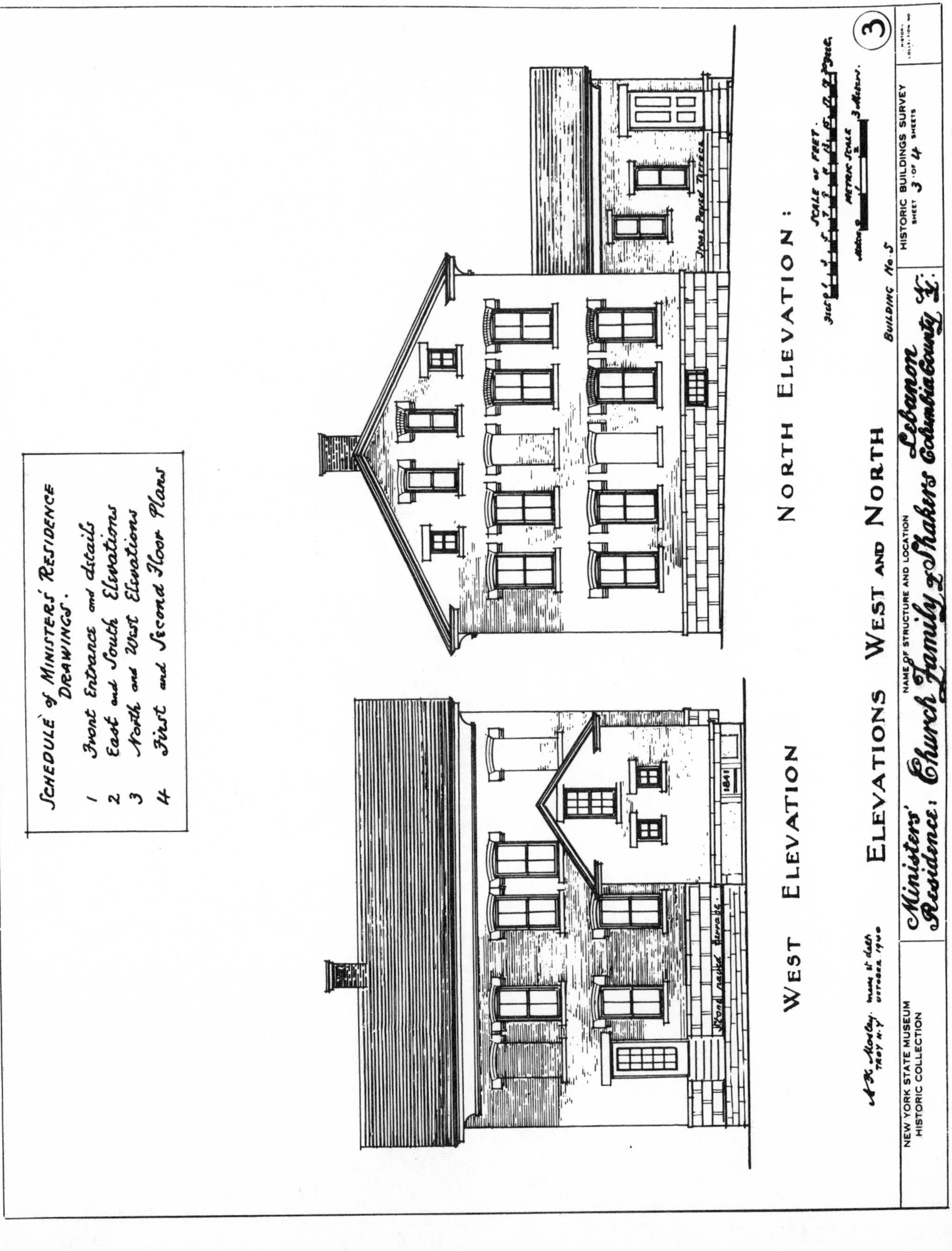

Schedule of Ministers' Residence
Drawings.

1 Front Entrance and details
2 East and South Elevations
3 North and West Elevations
4 First and Second Floor Plans

WEST ELEVATION

NORTH ELEVATION:

ELEVATIONS WEST AND NORTH

Ministers' Residence: Church Family of Shakers Lebanon Columbia County N.Y.

HISTORIC BUILDINGS SURVEY
SHEET 3 OF 4 SHEETS

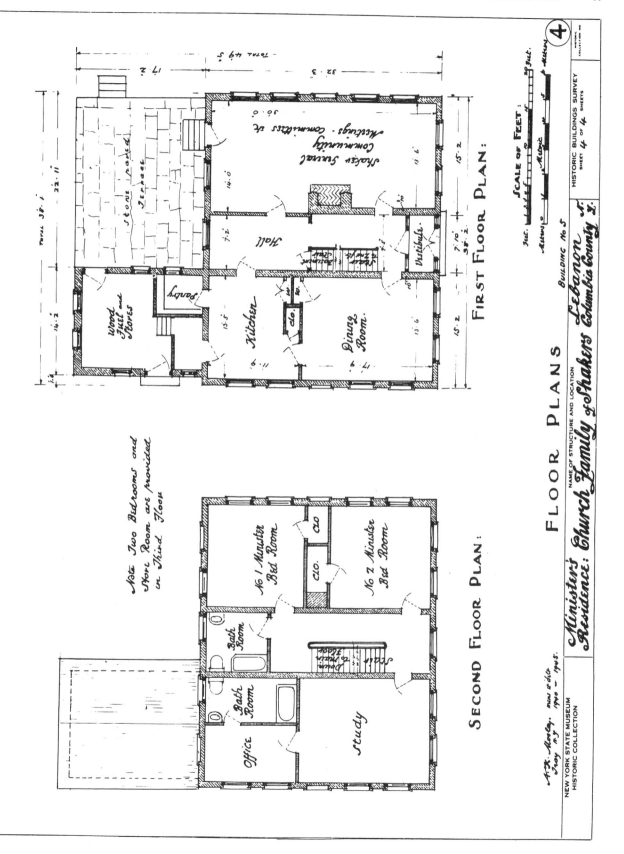

FIRST FLOOR PLAN:

Total 49.5

17.2

32.3

36.0

Shaker Sacred Community Meetings · Committees etc.

Stone paved Furnace

Wood Fuel and Stores

Pantry

Kitchen

Hall

Dining Room.

Vestibule.

Total 38.1

22.11

14.2

15.5

14.0

13.6

15.2

7.2

7.10

SECOND FLOOR PLAN:

Note Two Bedrooms and Store Room are provided in Third Floor

No 1 Minister Bed Room

No 2 Minister Bed Room

CLO

CLO.

Bath Room

Bath Room

Office

Study

FLOOR PLANS

NAME OF STRUCTURE AND LOCATION

Ministers Residence: Church Family of Shakers Lebanon Columbia County N.

BUILDING No 5

SCALE OF FEET:

HISTORIC BUILDINGS SURVEY
SHEET 4 OF 4 SHEETS

4

NEW YORK STATE MUSEUM
HISTORIC COLLECTION

BLACKSMITH'S SHOP: CHURCH FAMILY
MOUNT LEBANON, NEW YORK

This two-story and basement building is of native limestone. It has a plastered roof cove, like that found in many Shaker buildings. The twin chimney flues are unique.

The water-wheel pit measures six feet nine inches wide to eighteen feet deep. It reaches from the subterranean level to the ceiling of the basement.

On the outside wall, over the first floor windows, are cast-iron numerals which give the date of construction as 1846.

Blacksmith's Shop

In the Blacksmith's Shop

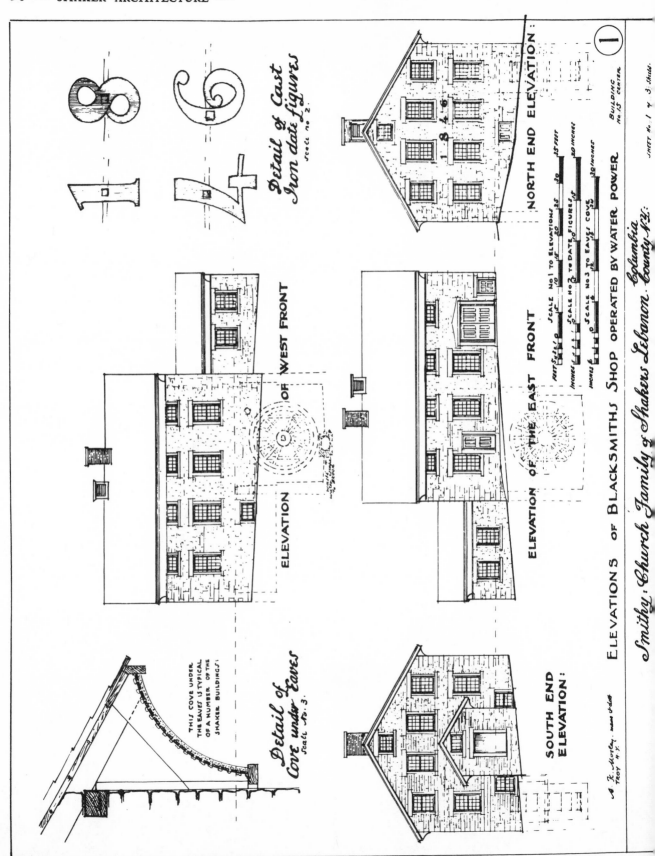

Detail of Cast
Iron date figures
SCALE NO 2.

NORTH END ELEVATION:

ELEVATION OF THE WEST FRONT

ELEVATION OF THE EAST FRONT

Detail of
Cove under Eaves
SCALE No. 3.

THIS COVE UNDER
THE EAVES IS TYPICAL
OF A NUMBER OF THE
SHAKER BUILDINGS:

SOUTH END
ELEVATION:

ELEVATIONS OF BLACKSMITHS SHOP OPERATED BY WATER POWER.

Smithy; Church Family of Shakers Lebanon, Columbia County, N.Y.

BUILDING No 13 CENTER.

SHEET No. 1 of 3 SHEETS.

A. R. Shirley, New York
TROY N.Y.

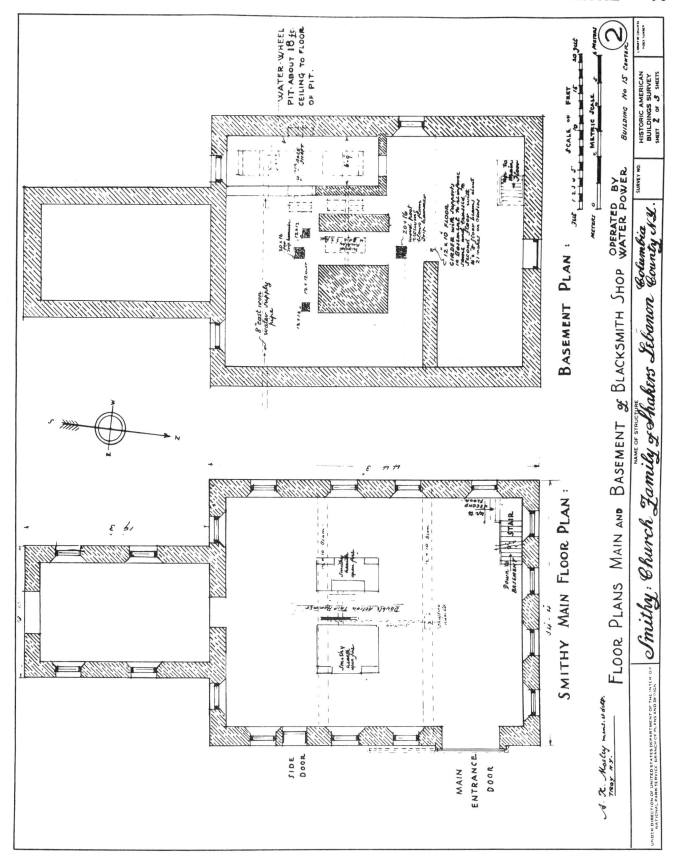

BASEMENT PLAN:

WATER-WHEEL PIT ABOUT 18 ft. CEILING TO FLOOR OF PIT.

SMITHY MAIN FLOOR PLAN:

SIDE DOOR

MAIN ENTRANCE DOOR

A. K. Mosby mes. v del.
TROY, N.Y.

FLOOR PLANS MAIN AND BASEMENT OF BLACKSMITH SHOP OPERATED BY WATER POWER.

NAME OF STRUCTURE
Smithy: Church Family of Shakers Lebanon, Columbia County, N.Y.

SURVEY NO.

HISTORIC AMERICAN BUILDINGS SURVEY
BUILDING No 15 CENTER.
SHEET 2 OF 3 SHEETS

LIBRARY OF CONGRESS
INDEX NUMBER

2

SCALE OF FEET

METRIC SCALE

UNDER DIRECTION OF UNITED STATES DEPARTMENT OF THE INTERIOR
NATIONAL PARK SERVICE BRANCH OF PLANS AND DESIGN.

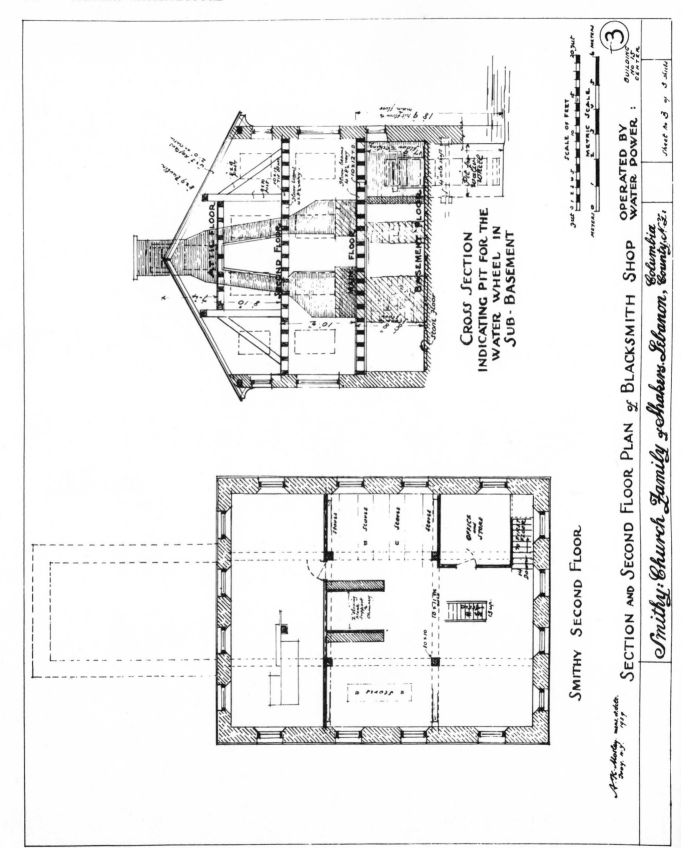

CROSS SECTION
INDICATING PIT FOR THE
WATER WHEEL IN
SUB-BASEMENT

SMITHY SECOND FLOOR

SECTION AND SECOND FLOOR PLAN of BLACKSMITH SHOP   OPERATED BY
WATER POWER :

Smithy: Church Family of Shakers. Lebanon, Columbia County, N.Y.

SHAKER SCHOOL: CHURCH FAMILY,
MOUNT LEBANON, NEW YORK

Erected in 1839, this Shaker building at one time served as a school for the six "families," or groups, in the Mount Lebanon Shaker village. From the foundation to the second floor the schoolhouse is made of irregular limestone blocks. It has upper and lower classrooms. The overhanging door canopy of the front entrance is duplicated over the rear door, which is the entrance to second-floor classroom.

Shaker School

The Schoolmaster and His Pupils

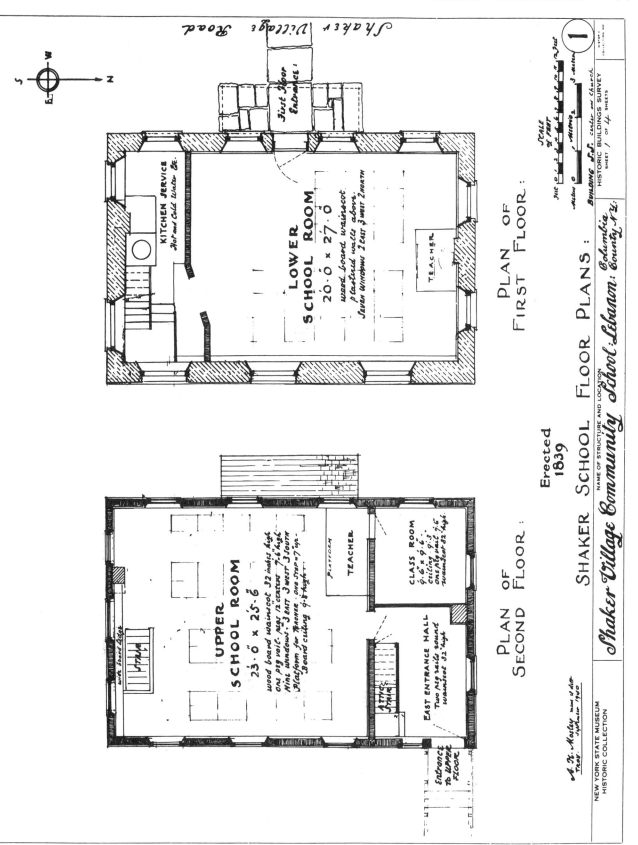

Shaker Village Community School: Lebanon: Columbia County: N.Y.:

SHAKER SCHOOL FLOOR PLANS:

Erected 1839

PLAN OF FIRST FLOOR:

PLAN OF SECOND FLOOR:

KITCHEN SERVICE
Hot and Cold Water Etc.

LOWER SCHOOL ROOM
20.0 x 27.0
wood board wainscot
plastered walls above.
SEVEN WINDOWS 2 EAST 3 WEST 2 NORTH

TEACHER

UPPER SCHOOL ROOM
23.0 x 25.6
wood board wainscot 32 inches high
one peg rail. Peg 12 inches 7.6 high.
Nine windows: 3 East 3 West 3 South
Platform for Teacher one step 7" up.
Board cutting 9.8 high.

with board edge

STAIRS

PLATFORM
TEACHER

CLASS ROOM
9.6 x 9.6.
ceiling 9.8.
one peg rail 7.6
wainscot 32 high.

ATTIC STAIRS

EAST ENTRANCE HALL
Two peg rails round
wainscot 32 high.

Entrance to UPPER FLOOR

First Floor Entrance:

Shaker Village Road

A.K. Mosley mus't del
Trac't   September 1940

NAME OF STRUCTURE AND LOCATION

BUILDING S.S. Center and Church

HISTORIC BUILDINGS SURVEY
SHEET 1 OF 4 SHEETS

SCALE of FEET

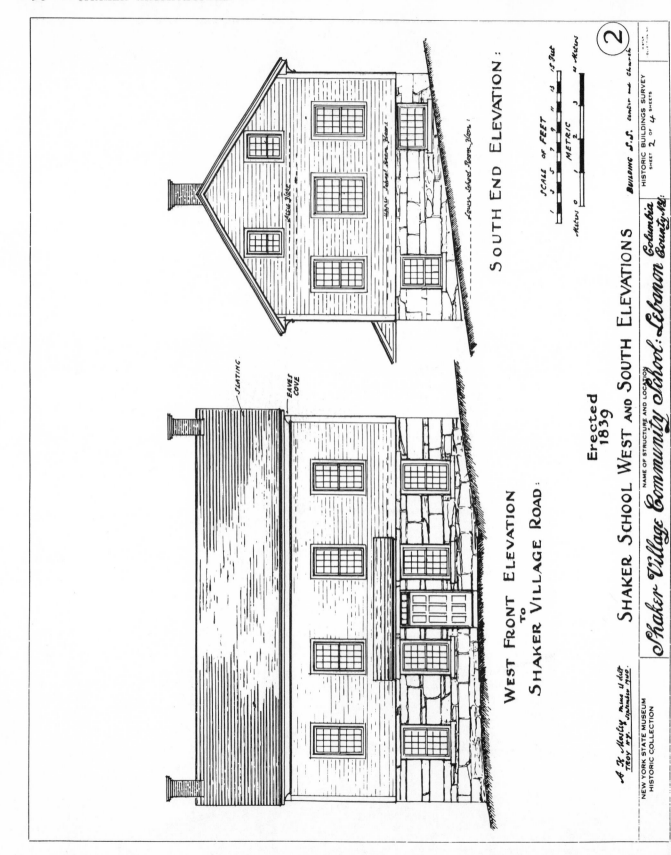

SOUTH END ELEVATION:

SCALE OF FEET

METRIC

②

WEST FRONT ELEVATION
TO
SHAKER VILLAGE ROAD:

Erected
1839

SHAKER SCHOOL WEST AND SOUTH ELEVATIONS

Shaker Village Community School: Lebanon Columbia County N.Y.

BUILDING S.S. center and church

HISTORIC BUILDINGS SURVEY
SHEET 2 OF 4 SHEETS

NAME OF STRUCTURE AND LOCATION

A. K. Morley mens U dept
Troy N.Y. September 1940.

NEW YORK STATE MUSEUM
HISTORIC COLLECTION

SLATING

EAVES
COVE

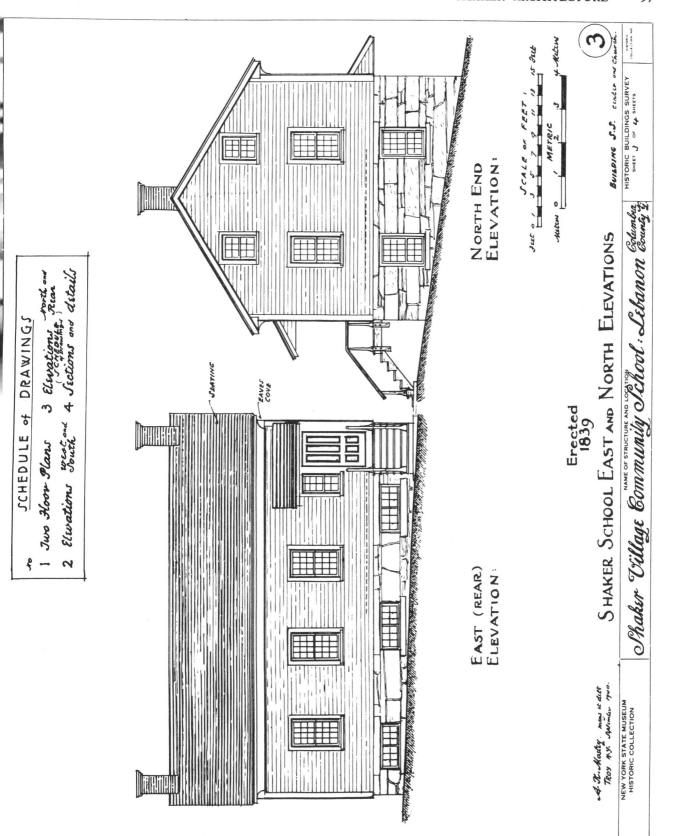

SCHEDULE of DRAWINGS

1 Two Floor Plans
3 Elevations North and Rear (Enclosure)
2 Elevations West and South
4 Sections and details

SHEATHING

EAVES COVE

NORTH END ELEVATION:

SCALE or FEET
Feet 0 1 3 5 7 9 11 13 15 Feet
METRIC
Metro 0 1 2 3 4 Metro

③

BUILDING S.S. Center and Church.

HISTORIC BUILDINGS SURVEY
SHEET 3 OF 4 SHEETS

HISTORIC COLLECTION NO.

EAST (REAR) ELEVATION:

Erected 1839

SHAKER SCHOOL EAST AND NORTH ELEVATIONS

NAME OF STRUCTURE AND LOCATION

Shaker Village Community School: Lebanon Columba County L.

A.F. Mosty, mea it dtt
Troy N.Y. Spring 1940.

NEW YORK STATE MUSEUM
HISTORIC COLLECTION

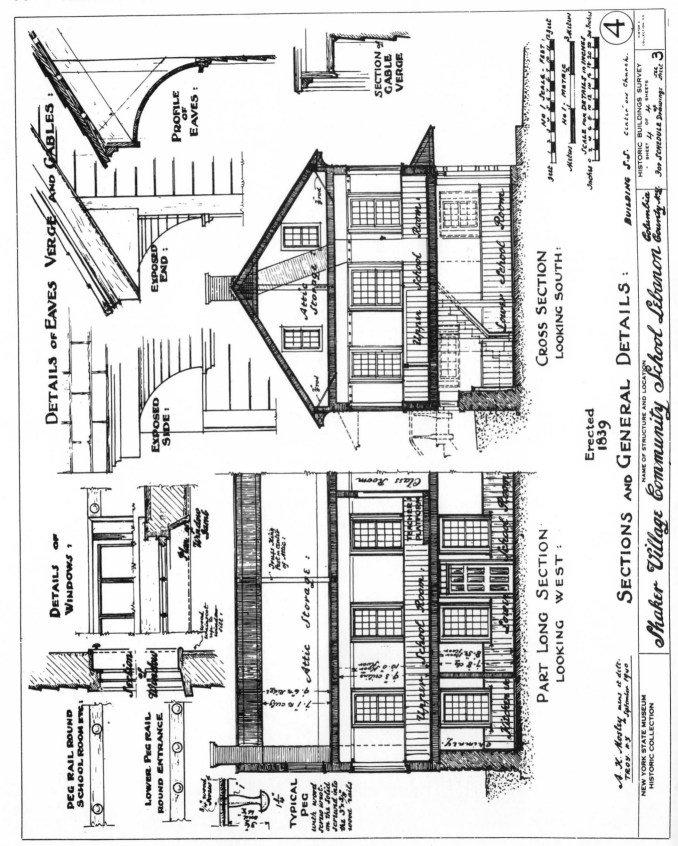

SISTERS' WORKSHOP: SOUTH FAMILY
MOUNT LEBANON, NEW YORK

The irregular limestone wall, up to the second floor, is covered with a smooth-finish cement coat. The eight-point, curved doorway is an unusual and beautiful feature in Shaker architecture. The off-center double doors are framed by this arch. The remainder of the building is of wood.

Sisters' Workshop

On the left of the main entrance is the dairy room with special arch kettles and sinks; on the right is the laundry with its battery of arch kettles. An unbroken stair rail runs from the first floor to the attic.

The carved stone over the front entrance gives the date of construction as 1851.

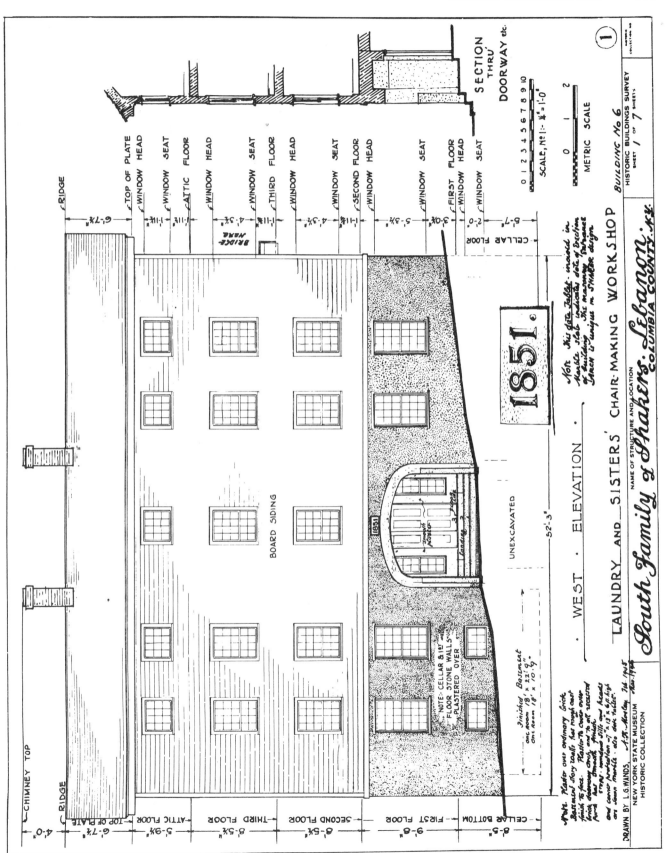

SECTION THRU' DOORWAY etc.

RIDGE
TOP OF PLATE
WINDOW HEAD
WINDOW SEAT
ATTIC FLOOR
WINDOW HEAD
WINDOW SEAT
THIRD FLOOR
WINDOW HEAD
WINDOW SEAT
SECOND FLOOR
WINDOW HEAD
WINDOW SEAT
FIRST FLOOR
WINDOW HEAD
WINDOW SEAT
CELLAR FLOOR

BRICK AREA

SCALE, No.1 :- ¼" = 1'-0"

0 1 2 3 4 5 6 7 8 9 10

METRIC SCALE

0 1 2

BUILDING No 6

HISTORIC BUILDINGS SURVEY

SHEET 1 OF 7 SHEETS

1851.

· WEST · ELEVATION ·

LAUNDRY AND SISTERS' CHAIR-MAKING WORKSHOP

NAME OF STRUCTURE AND LOCATION

South Family of Shakers, Lebanon,
COLUMBIA COUNTY, N.Y.

DRAWN BY L.G.WINDS, A.R.Morley, Feb.1945, Mar.1945

NEW YORK STATE MUSEUM
HISTORIC COLLECTION

CHIMNEY TOP
RIDGE
TOP OF PLATE
ATTIC FLOOR
THIRD FLOOR
SECOND FLOOR
FIRST FLOOR
CELLAR BOTTOM

BOARD SIDING

UNEXCAVATED

52'-3"

NOTE: CELLAR & 1ST
FLOOR STONE WALLS
PLASTERED OVER

Finished Basement
one room 18' x 22' 9"
one room 18' x 10' 9"

1851

landing 2

Smooth Mortar
landing 3

Note: Plaster over ordinary brick.
Exterior story walls has rough cast
finish to face. Plaster 7/8 coats over
brick shows sanded finish. Interior
fine wood-grained sills and heads
that: wooden sills and heads
and corner construction-2"x12"x6" high
on down mantle- also dark trailer.

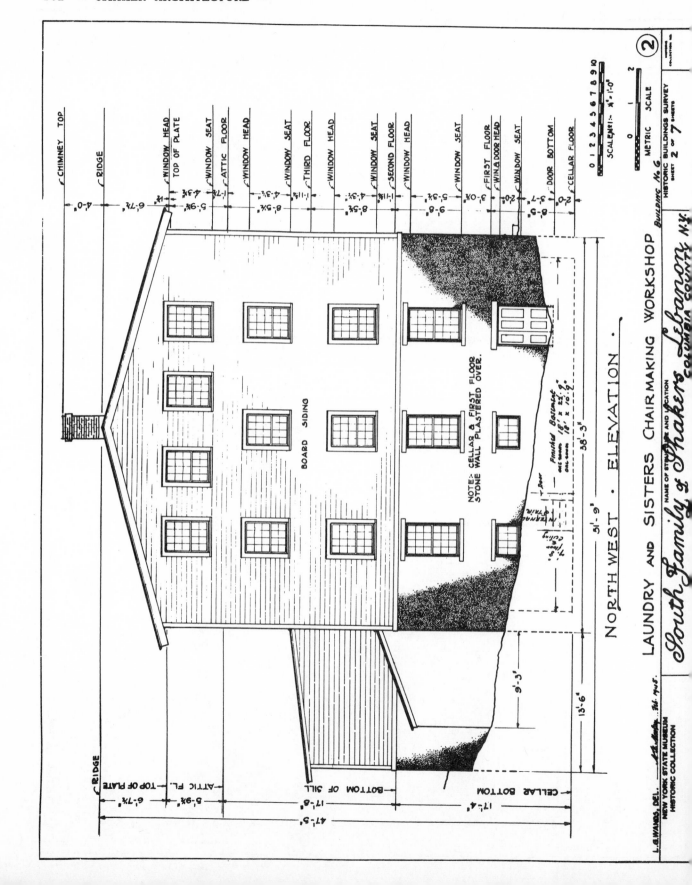

NORTH WEST · ELEVATION ·

LAUNDRY AND SISTERS CHAIRMAKING WORKSHOP

South Family of Shakers Lebanon
COLUMBIA COUNTY N.Y.

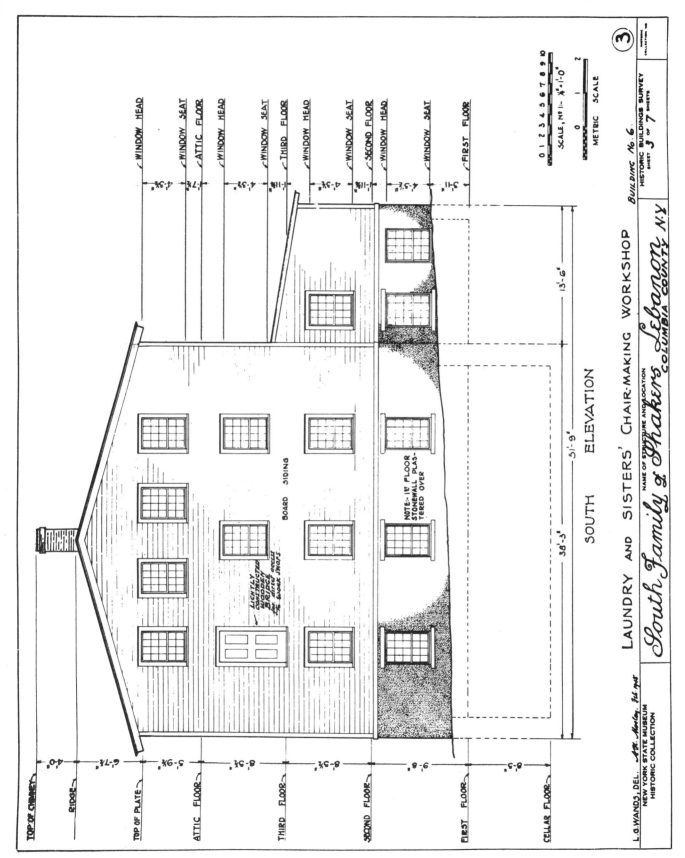

LAUNDRY AND SISTERS' CHAIR-MAKING WORKSHOP

SOUTH ELEVATION

South Family of Shakers Lebanon COLUMBIA COUNTY N.Y.

NAME OF STRUCTURE AND LOCATION

BUILDING No. 6.

HISTORIC BUILDINGS SURVEY
SHEET 3 OF 7 SHEETS

L.G. WANDS, DEL.   A.R. Morley, Feb. 1938
NEW YORK STATE MUSEUM
HISTORIC COLLECTION

SCALE, No. 1:— ⅜" = 1'-0"

METRIC SCALE

0 1 2 3 4 5 6 7 8 9 10

0   1   2

③

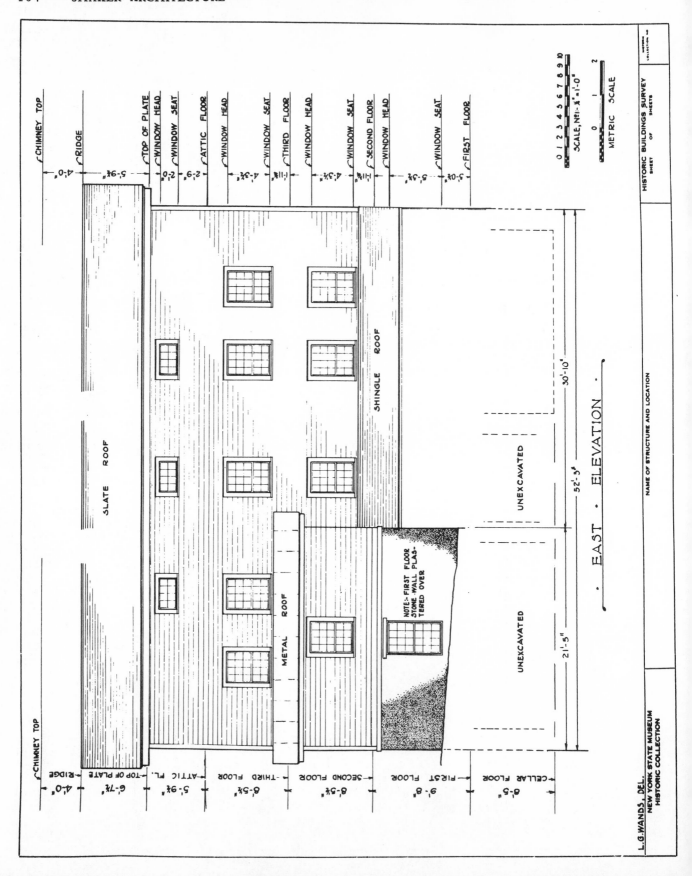

· EAST · ELEVATION ·

SLATE ROOF

SHINGLE ROOF

METAL ROOF

UNEXCAVATED

UNEXCAVATED

NOTE:- FIRST FLOOR STONE·WALL PLAS- TERED OVER

CHIMNEY TOP
RIDGE
TOP OF PLATE
WINDOW HEAD
WINDOW SEAT
ATTIC FLOOR
WINDOW HEAD
WINDOW SEAT
THIRD FLOOR
WINDOW HEAD
WINDOW SEAT
SECOND FLOOR
WINDOW HEAD
WINDOW SEAT
FIRST FLOOR

CHIMNEY TOP
RIDGE
TOP OF PLATE
ATTIC FL.
THIRD FLOOR
SECOND FLOOR
FIRST FLOOR
CELLAR FLOOR

SCALE, NºI- ¼"=1'-0"
METRIC SCALE

HISTORIC BUILDINGS SURVEY
SHEET OF SHEETS

NAME OF STRUCTURE AND LOCATION

L.G.WANDS. DEL.
NEW YORK STATE MUSEUM
HISTORIC COLLECTION

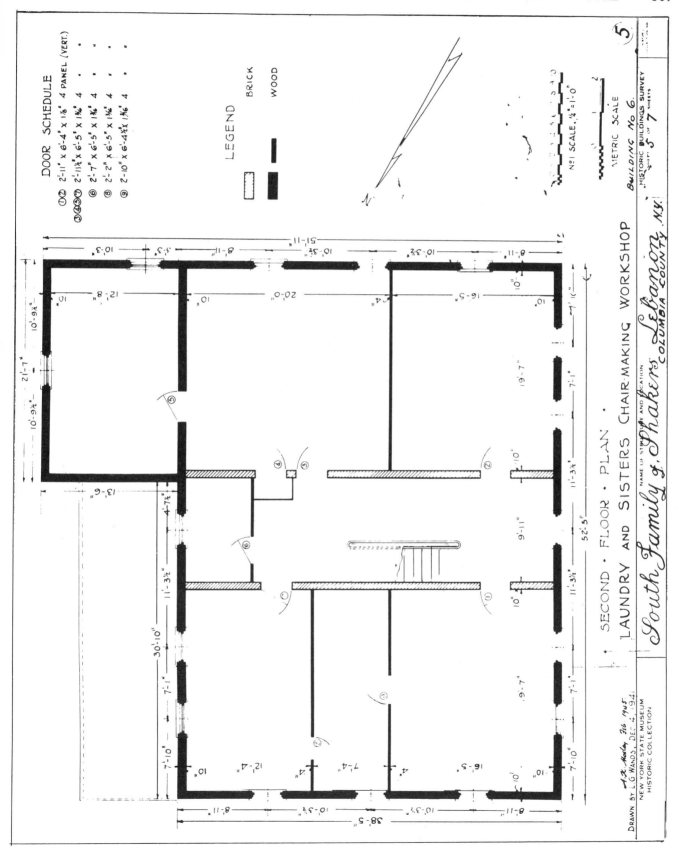

DOOR SCHEDULE

① ② 2'-11" x 6'-4" x 1⅛" 4 PANEL (VERT.)
③④⑤⑦ 2'-11½" x 6'-5" x 1¾" 4   "
⑥ 2'-7" x 6'-5" x 1¾" 4   "
⑧ 2'-2" x 6'-5" x 1¾" 4   "
⑨ 2'-10" x 6'-4¼" x 1⅞" 4   "

LEGEND

BRICK

WOOD

Nº1 SCALE ¼" = 1'-0"

METRIC SCALE

BUILDING Nº 6.

HISTORIC BUILDINGS SURVEY

SHEET 5 OF 7 SHEETS

· SECOND · FLOOR · PLAN ·

LAUNDRY AND SISTERS CHAIR·MAKING WORKSHOP

South Family of Shakers Lebanon

COLUMBIA COUNTY, N.Y.

NAME OF STRUCTURE AND LOCATION

DRAWN BY L.G. WANDS, DEC 4, 1941

NEW YORK STATE MUSEUM
HISTORIC COLLECTION

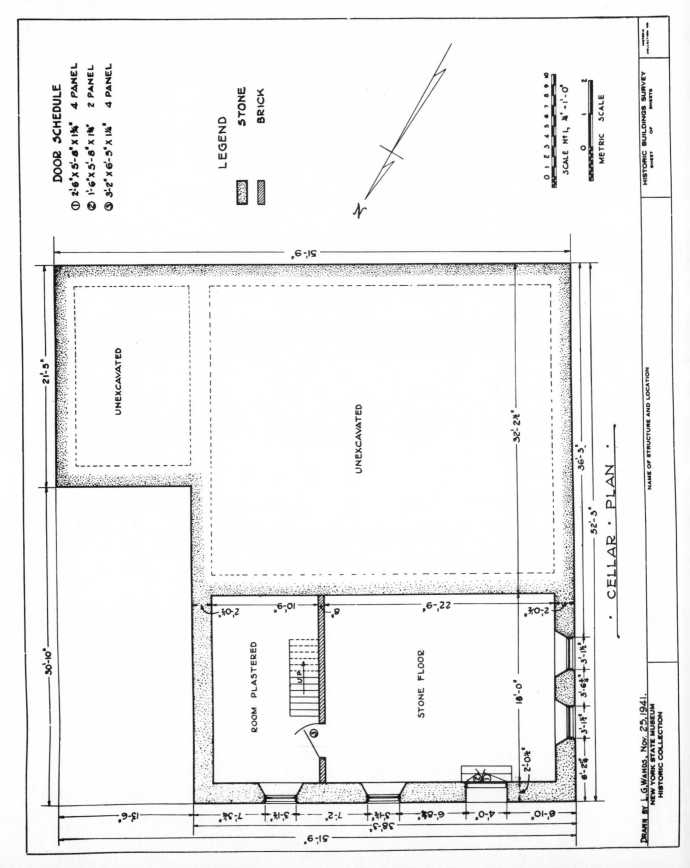

DOOR SCHEDULE
① 2'-6" x 5'-8" x 1⅜" 4 PANEL
② 1'-6" x 5'-8" x 1⅜" 2 PANEL
③ 3'-2" x 6'-5" x 1⅜" 4 PANEL

LEGEND
STONE
BRICK

SCALE Nº 1, ¼"=1'-0"

METRIC SCALE

HISTORIC BUILDINGS SURVEY
SHEET OF SHEETS

NAME OF STRUCTURE AND LOCATION

· CELLAR · PLAN ·

UNEXCAVATED

UNEXCAVATED

ROOM PLASTERED

UP

STONE FLOOR

DRAWN BY L.G.WANDS, Nov. 25, 1941.
NEW YORK STATE MUSEUM
HISTORIC COLLECTION

51'-9"
21'-5"
30'-10"
32'-2¼"
36'-3"
52'-3"
13'-6"
6'-2¼"
38'-3"
51'-9"
18'-0"
2'-10¾"
10'-9"
8"
22'-9"
2'-10¾"
3'-1¼"
3'-6¼"
3'-1¼"
2'-0¾"
6'-10"
4'-0"
6'-8¼"
3'-1¼"
7'-2"
3'-1¼"
7'-3¾"

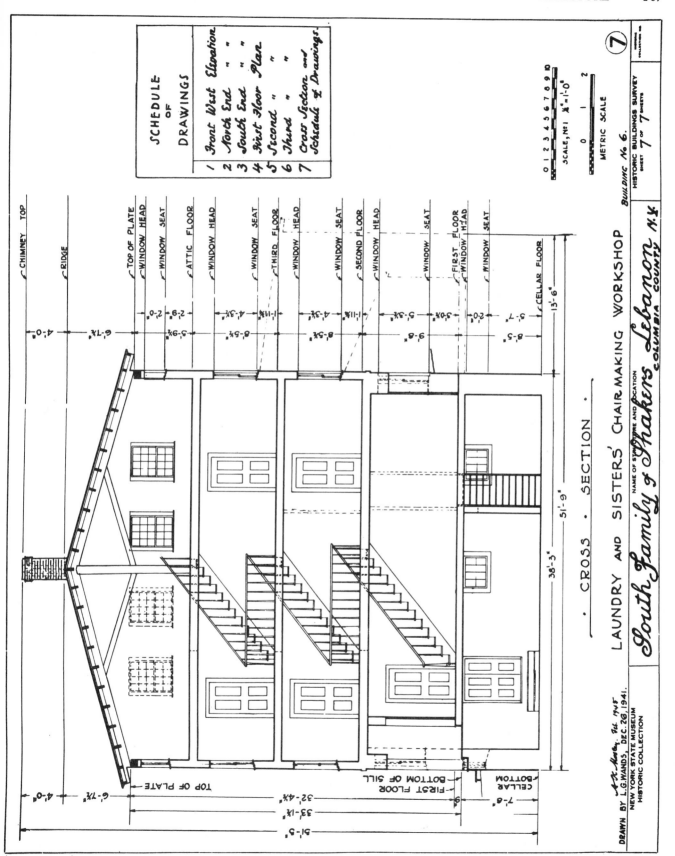

SCHEDULE OF DRAWINGS

1 Front West Elevation
2 North End   "   "
3 South End   "   "
4 First Floor Plan
5 Second   "   "
6 Third   "   "
7 Cross Section and Schedule of Drawings.

SCALE, No. 1 ¼" = 1'-0"

0 1 2 3 4 5 6 7 8 9 10

METRIC SCALE

0   1   2

BUILDING No. 6.

HISTORIC BUILDINGS SURVEY
SHEET 7 OF 7 SHEETS

· CROSS · SECTION ·

LAUNDRY AND SISTERS' CHAIRMAKING WORKSHOP

NAME OF STRUCTURE AND LOCATION

South Family of Shakers Lebanon N.Y.
COLUMBIA COUNTY

DRAWN BY L. G. WANDS, DEC. 26, 1941.
NEW YORK STATE MUSEUM
HISTORIC COLLECTION

CHIMNEY TOP
RIDGE
TOP OF PLATE
WINDOW HEAD
WINDOW SEAT
ATTIC FLOOR
WINDOW HEAD
WINDOW SEAT
THIRD FLOOR
WINDOW HEAD
WINDOW SEAT
SECOND FLOOR
WINDOW HEAD
WINDOW SEAT
FIRST FLOOR
WINDOW HEAD
WINDOW SEAT
CELLAR FLOOR

TOP OF PLATE
FIRST FLOOR
BOTTOM OF SILL
CELLAR BOTTOM

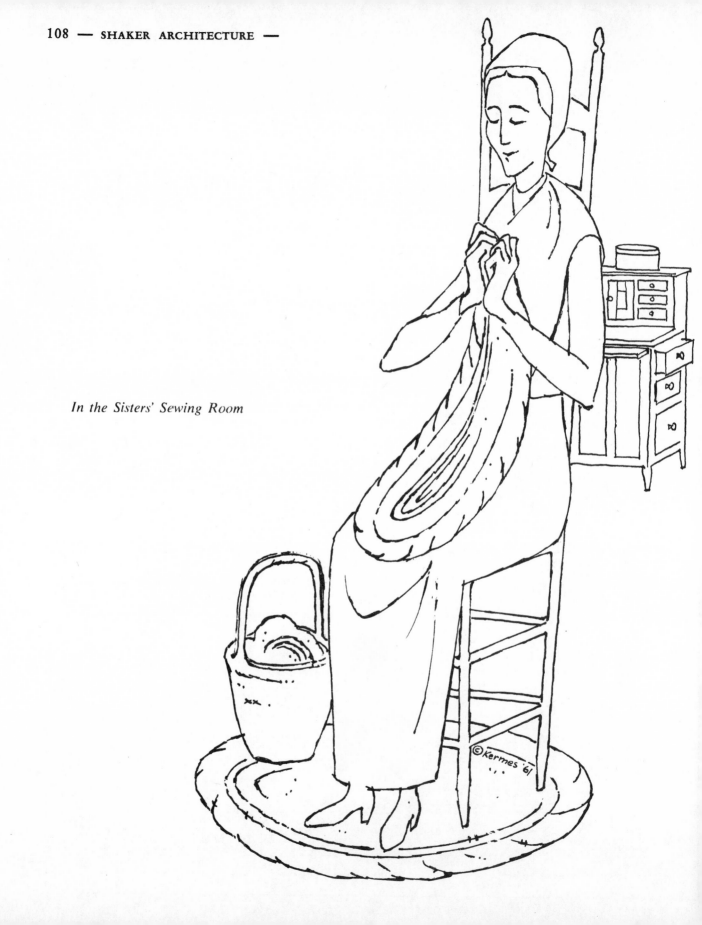

In the Sisters' Sewing Room

MAIN DWELLING HOUSE: WEST FAMILY
WATERVLIET, NEW YORK

A painted strip of tin, on the upper floor of this building and over the stairs, gives the date of construction as 1828. Of all the Shaker buildings still remaining at Watervliet (Niskayuna), New York, this is perhaps the most typical example of Shaker architectural design. There are three main floors: an attic, a basement, and a storage cellar.

In the basement are the kitchen, bakeroom, dining room, and food storage rooms or pantries.

On the second floor of the rear extension is the Family Meeting Room. In the attics of both the main structure and this extension are built-in chests

Main Dwelling House

of drawers for the storage of clothing and bedding, and a special arrangement of peg boards to hold clothing and hats.

The retiring rooms, or bedrooms, are identical on all floors of the main portion of the structure. The original hand-forged hardware on all the doors is still intact. All woodwork, built-in cupboards, and built-in chests of drawers remain in pristine condition.

Surmounting the slate roof of the main portion of the building is a bell tower approximately 6 feet high and 4 feet square. This bell summoned the members at rising time (4:30 A.M. during the summer and autumn months, and 5:30 A.M. during the winter months), and to the three meals of the day.

The building is of red brick on a foundation of irregular slabs of field stone. The window arches are of brick, and the window sills of limestone.

Off-Center Double Doors

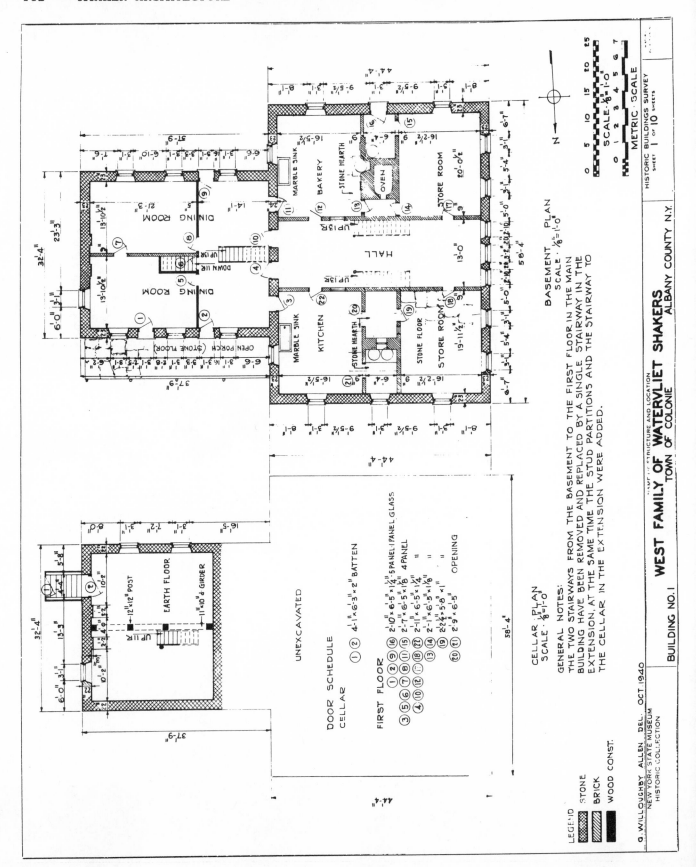

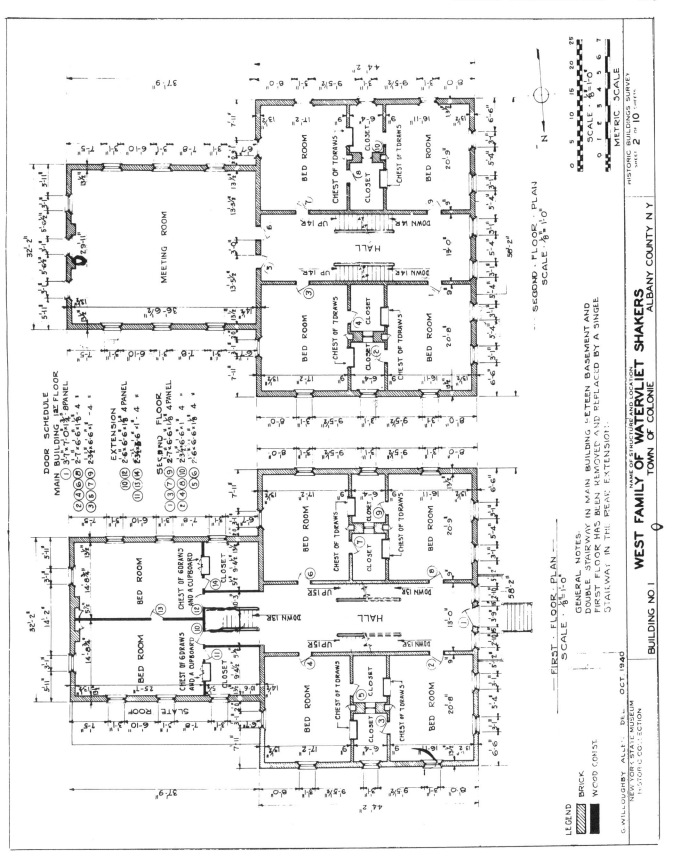

— FIRST · FLOOR · PLAN —
SCALE · 1/8"=1'-0"

— SECOND · FLOOR · PLAN —
SCALE · 1/8"=1'-0"

DOOR SCHEDULE

MAIN BUILDING 1ST FLOOR
① 3'-7"×7'-0"×1¾" 8PANEL
② ④ ⑥ ⑧ 2'-7"×6'-6"×1¾" - 4 "
③ ⑤ ⑦ ⑨ 2'-3"×6'-6"×1¾" - 4 "

EXTENSION
⑩ ⑫ 2'-6"×6'-6"×1¾" 4 PANEL
⑪ ⑬ ⑭ 2'-3"×6'-6"×1¾" - 4 "

SECOND FLOOR
① ③ ⑦ ⑨ 2'-7"×6'-6"×1¾" 4 PANEL
② ④ ⑧ ⑩ 2'-3"×6'-6"×1¾" 4 "
⑤ ⑥ 2'-6"×6'-6"×1¾" 4 "

GENERAL NOTES.
DOUBLE STAIRWAY IN MAIN BUILDING BETWEEN BASEMENT AND
FIRST FLOOR HAS BEEN REMOVED AND REPLACED BY A SINGLE
STAIRWAY IN THE REAR EXTENSION.

LEGEND
▨ BRICK
■ WOOD CONST.

NAME OF STRUCTURE AND LOCATION
WEST FAMILY OF WATERVLIET SHAKERS
TOWN OF COLONIE   ALBANY COUNTY N.Y.

BUILDING NO. 1

G. WILLOUGHBY ALLEN DEL   OCT. 1940
NEW YORK STATE MUSEUM
HISTORIC COLLECTION

HISTORIC BUILDINGS SURVEY
SHEET 2 OF 10 SHEETS

SCALE · 1/8"=1'-0"
0   5   10   15   20   25

METRIC SCALE
0 1 2 3 4 5 6 7

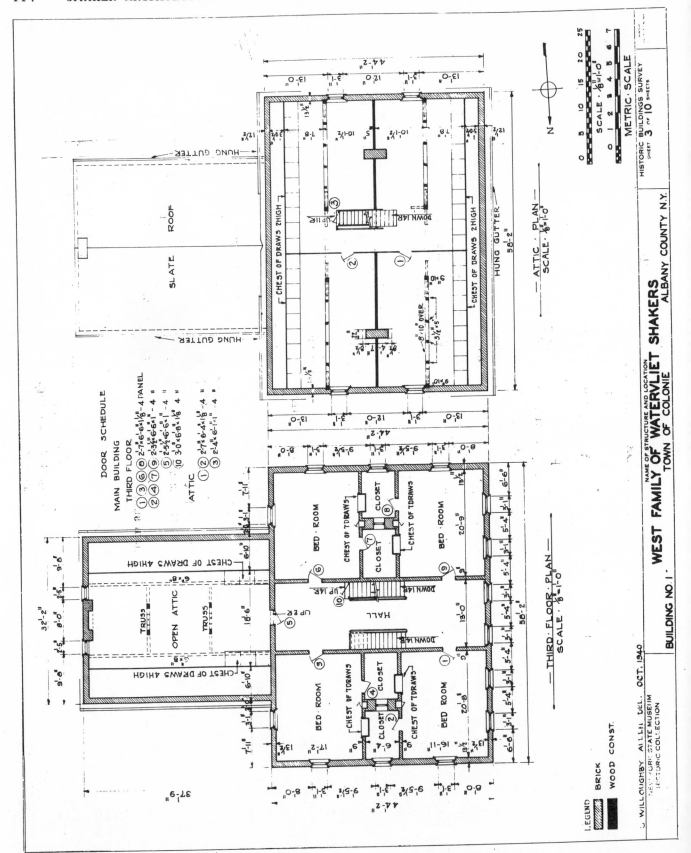

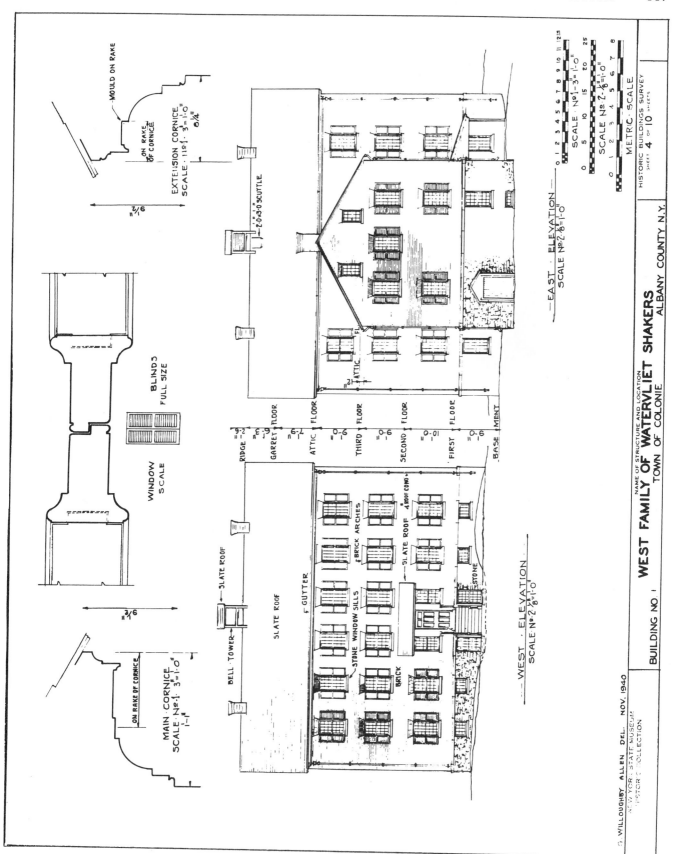

MOULD ON RAKE

ON RAKE OF CORNICE

EXTENSION CORNICE
SCALE : 1½"·1'·3"=1'·0"
6¼"

9¼"

MAIN·CORNICE·
SCALE·N°1· 3"=1'·0"
1'·1"

ON RAKE OF CORNICE

BLINDS
FULL SIZE

WINDOW
SCALE

9/16"

3/16"

SCUTTLE

2'·0·3·0

ATTIC FL.

RIDGE 9'·2"

GARRET FLOOR 9'·3"

ATTIC FLOOR 8'·1"

THIRD FLOOR 10'·6"

SECOND FLOOR 10'·6"

FIRST FLOOR 10'·0½"

BASEMENT 10'·6"

—EAST·ELEVATION—
SCALE N°2 ⅛"=1'·0"

SLATE ROOF

BELL TOWER

SLATE ROOF

GUTTER

STONE WINDOW SILLS

BRICK ARCHES

BRICK

SLATE ROOF

ROOF CONDR

STONE ARCHES

STONE

—WEST·ELEVATION—
SCALE N°2 ⅛"=1'·0"

SCALE N°1·3"=1'·0"
0 1 2 3 4 5 6 7 8 9 10 11 12½
0 5 10 15 20 25

SCALE N°2·⅛"=1'·0"
0 1 2 3 4 5 6 7 8

METRIC·SCALE

HISTORIC BUILDINGS SURVEY
SHEET 4 OF 10 SHEETS

NAME OF STRUCTURE AND LOCATION
WEST FAMILY OF WATERVLIET SHAKERS
TOWN OF COLONIE   ALBANY COUNTY N.Y.

BUILDING NO. 1

G. WILLOUGHBY ALLEN DEL. NOV. 1940

NEW YORK STATE MUSEUM
HISTORY COLLECTION

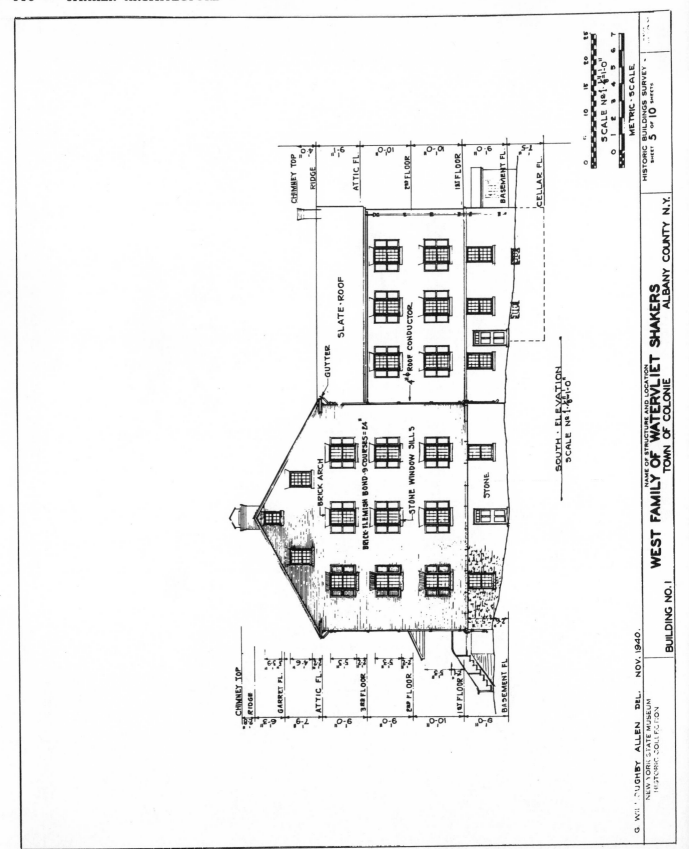

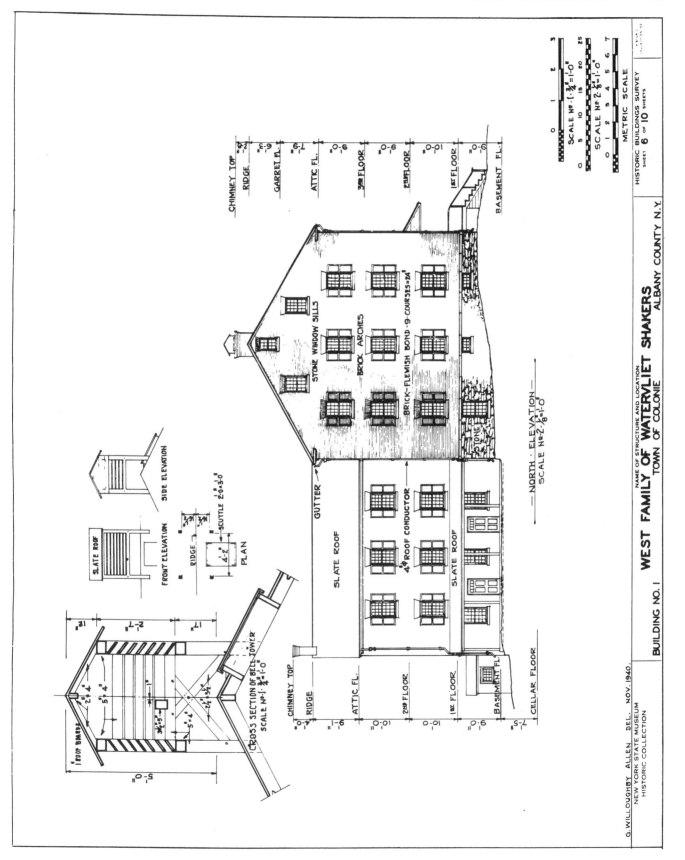

WEST FAMILY OF WATERVLIET SHAKERS
TOWN OF COLONIE   ALBANY COUNTY N.Y.

BUILDING NO. I

NAME OF STRUCTURE AND LOCATION

G. WILLOUGHBY ALLEN DEL. NOV. 1940.
NEW YORK STATE MUSEUM
HISTORIC COLLECTION

HISTORIC BUILDINGS SURVEY
SHEET 6 OF 10 SHEETS

SCALE No.1 - ¾" = 1'-0"
SCALE No.2 - ⅛" = 1'-0"
METRIC SCALE

— NORTH · ELEVATION —
SCALE No.2 ⅛"=1'-0"

CHIMNEY TOP
RIDGE
GARRET FL.
ATTIC FL.
3RD FLOOR
2ND FLOOR
1ST FLOOR
BASEMENT FL.

STONE WINDOW SILLS
BRICK ARCHES
BRICK — FLEMISH BOND — 9 COURSES = 24"
STONE

GUTTER
SLATE ROOF
4" ROOF CONDUCTOR
SLATE ROOF

CHIMNEY TOP
RIDGE
ATTIC FL.
2ND FLOOR
1ST FLOOR
BASEMENT FL.
CELLAR FLOOR

SIDE ELEVATION
SLATE ROOF
FRONT ELEVATION
RIDGE
SCUTTLE 2'-0 x 3'-0
PLAN

CROSS SECTION OF BELL TOWER
SCALE No.1 ¾"=1'-0"
ROOF BOARDS

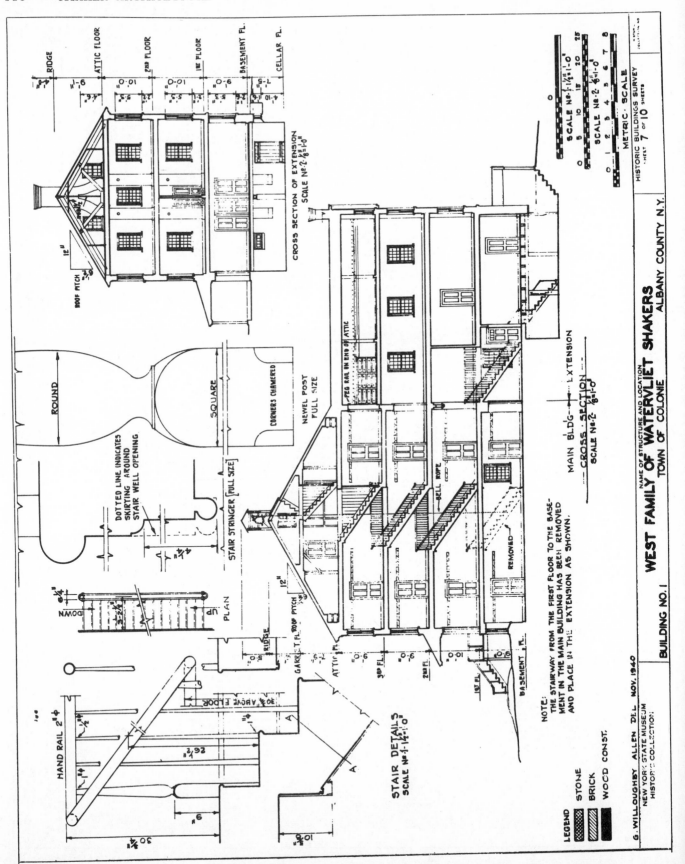

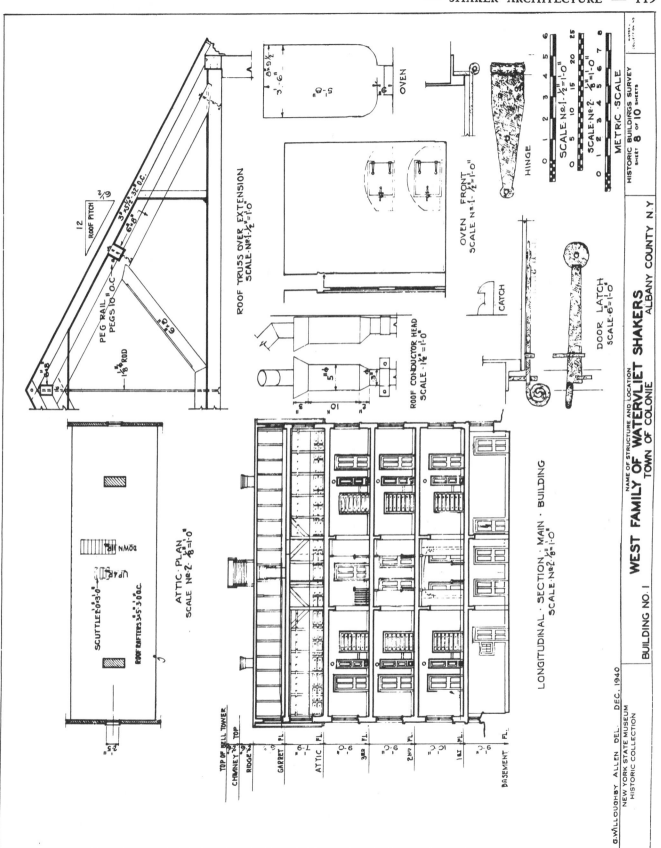

ROOF TRUSS OVER EXTENSION
SCALE·N̊1·1½"=1'-0"

ROOF PITCH
12
9

PEG RAIL 1" O.C.
PEGS 10" O.C.

OVEN

OVEN·FRONT
SCALE·N̊1·1½"=1'-0"

HINGE

METRIC·SCALE
SCALE·N̊1·1½"=1'-0"
SCALE·N̊2·6"=1'-0"

HISTORIC BUILDINGS SURVEY
SHEET 8 OF 10 SHEETS

ROOF CONDUCTOR HEAD
SCALE·1¼"=1'-0"

CATCH

DOOR LATCH
SCALE·6"=1'-0"

ATTIC·PLAN
SCALE·N̊2·⅛"=1'-0"

SCUTTLE 2'-0"×3'-0"
DOWN
UP
ROOF RAFTERS 3×5 3'-0" O.C.

LONGITUDINAL·SECTION·MAIN·BUILDING
SCALE·N̊2·⅛"=1'-0"

TOP OF BELL TOWER
CHIMNEY·TOP·TOP
RIDGE
GARRET·FL.
ATTIC·FL.
3RD·FL.
2ND·FL.
1ST·FL.
BASEMENT·FL.

WEST FAMILY OF WATERVLIET SHAKERS
ALBANY COUNTY N.Y.
TOWN OF COLONIE

NAME OF STRUCTURE AND LOCATION
BUILDING NO. I

G.WILLOUGHBY ALLEN DEL.   DEC. 1940
NEW YORK STATE MUSEUM
HISTORIC COLLECTION

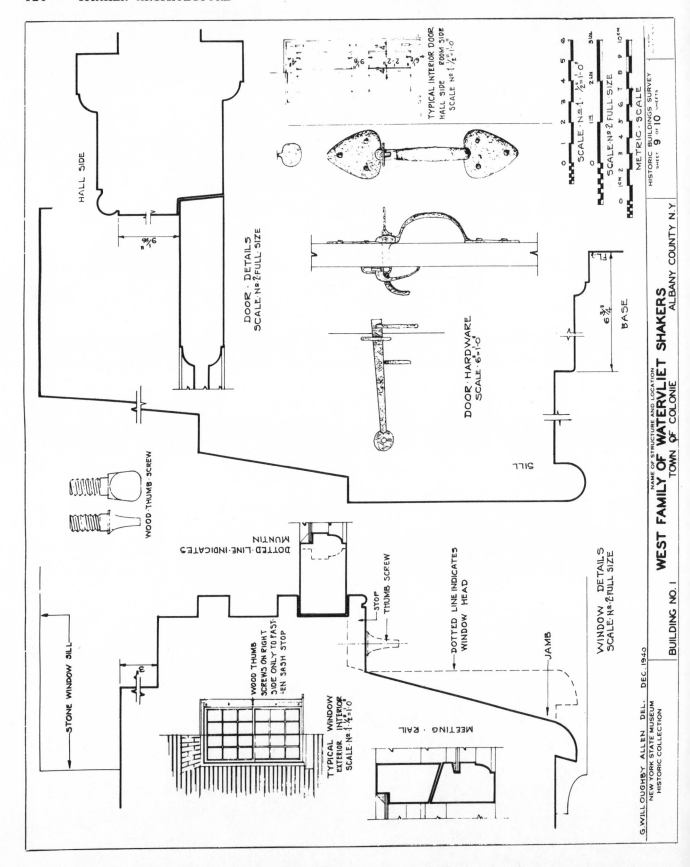

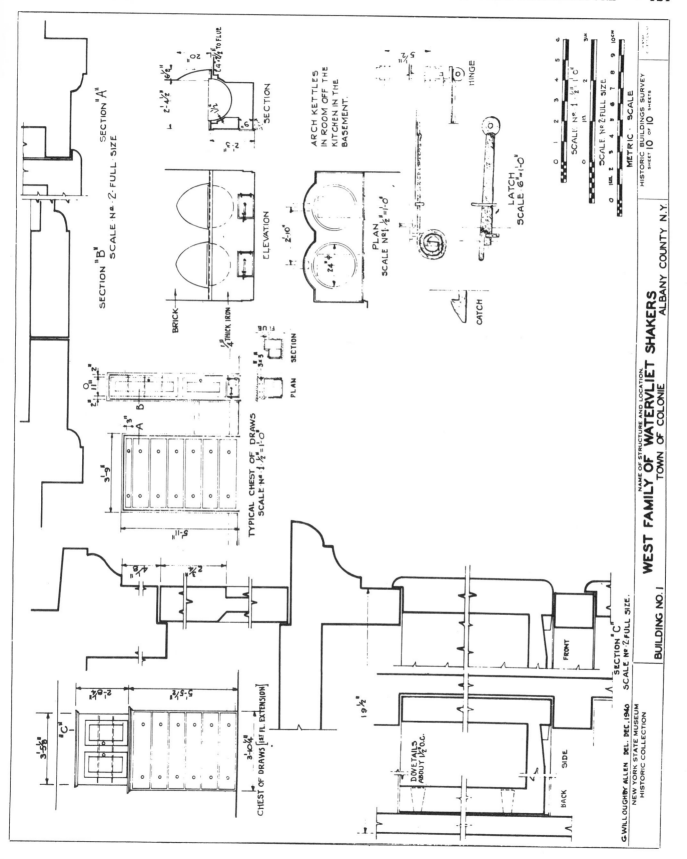

SECTION "A"
SCALE Nº 2 FULL SIZE

SECTION "B"
SCALE Nº 2 FULL SIZE

SECTION

BRICK

ELEVATION

¼" THICK IRON

FLUE

3 x 3

SECTION

PLAN

TYPICAL CHEST OF DRAWS
SCALE Nº 1 ½" = 1'-0"

ARCH KETTLES
IN ROOM OFF THE
KITCHEN IN THE
BASEMENT.

PLAN
SCALE Nº 1 ½"=1'-0"

HINGE

CATCH

LATCH
SCALE 6"=1'-0"

METRIC · SCALE
HISTORIC BUILDINGS SURVEY
SHEET 10 OF 10 SHEETS

SCALE Nº 1 · ½"·1'-0"

SCALE Nº 2 FULL SIZE

CHEST OF DRAWS

CHEST OF DRAWS [1ST FL. EXTENSION]

DOVETAILS
ABOUT 1½" O.C.

SECTION "C"
SCALE Nº 2 FULL SIZE.

FRONT

SIDE

BACK

NAME OF STRUCTURE AND LOCATION
WEST FAMILY OF WATERVLIET SHAKERS
TOWN OF COLONIE   ALBANY COUNTY N.Y.

BUILDING NO. 1

G. WILLOUGHBY ALLEN DEL. DEC. 1940
NEW YORK STATE MUSEUM
HISTORIC COLLECTION

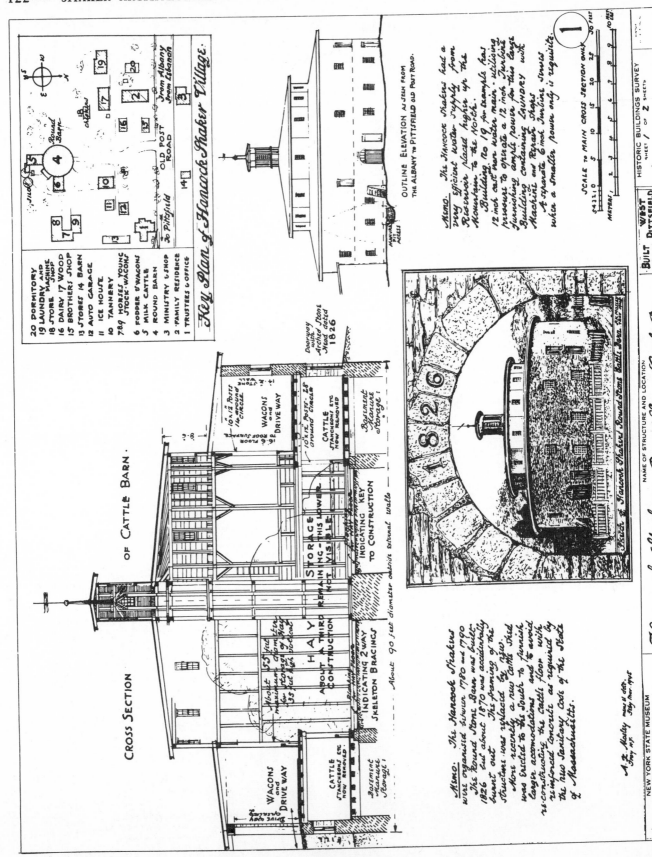

Key Plan of Hancock Shaker Village.

20 DORMITORY
19 LAUNDRY AND MACHINE SHOP
18 STORE SHOP
17 WOOD
16 DAIRY
15 BROTHERS SHOP
14 BARN
13 STORES
12 AUTO GARAGE
11 ICE HOUSE
10 TANNERY
7,8,9 HORSES, YOUNG STOCK, WAGONS
6 FODDER & WAGONS
5 MILK CATTLE
4 ROUND BARN
3 MINISTRY & SHOP
2 FAMILY RESIDENCE
1 TRUSTEES & OFFICE

OUTLINE ELEVATION as seen from THE ALBANY to PITTSFIELD OLD POST ROAD.

Memo. This Hancock Shakers had a very efficient water supply from Reservoir placed higher up the Mountain to the Notch.

Building No 19 for example has 12 inch cast iron water main - utilizing pressure to operate a 12 inch Turbine furnishing ample power for this large building containing LAUNDRY with Machine and Repair Shops.

At present 6 inch Turbine serves when a smaller power only is requisite.

SCALE to MAIN CROSS SECTION only.

HISTORIC BUILDINGS SURVEY
SHEET 1 OF 2 SHEETS

CROSS SECTION OF CATTLE BARN.

Doorway with Arched Stone Head dated 1826

10 x 12 Posts 14' around CIRCLE
WAGONS and DRIVE WAY
6'-6" FLOOR
10 x 11 Posts 22' around CIRCLE
CATTLE STANCHIONS ETC NOW REMOVED
Basement Manure Storage.

HAY STORAGE REMAINING - THIS LOWER NOT VISIBLE
INDICATING KEY TO CONSTRUCTION

About 55' indicating maximum diameter for storage of Hay.
33 feet high vertical.

About a third indicating 2 WAY CONSTRUCTION
Pitch indicating 2 WAY SKELETON BRACINGS.

About 90 feet diameter outside external walls.

WAGONS and DRIVE WAY
CATTLE STANCHIONS ETC. NOW REMOVED
Basement Manure Storage!
Drive way opening

Memo. The Hancock Shakers were organised between 1780 and 1790. This Round Stone Barn was built 1826, but about 1870 was accidentally burnt out. This framing of the structure was replaced by two.

More recently a new Cattle Shed was erected to the South to furnish large accomodations and to avoid re-constructing the cattle floor with reinforced concrete as required by the new sanitary code of the State of Massachusetts.

A.F. Morley, New York.

NEW YORK STATE MUSEUM
HISTORIC COLLECTION

NAME OF STRUCTURE AND LOCATION
Hancock Shakers Round Stone Cattle Barn
BUILT WEST PITTSFIELD MASS. 1826

Church & Hancock Shakers Round Stone Cattle Barn, Built Jan.

ROUND BARN: HANCOCK SHAKERS, WEST PITTSFIELD, MASSACHUSETTS

The stones of the large curved-arch doorway bear the date 1826. Tradition and Shaker folklore say that one of the brethren, who was wheelwright and cooper, suggested that this barn should have a circular floor plan. The floor plan and elevation of this W.P.A. drawing shows that there are three concentric elements and that they are of different heights.

The central, or the innermost, element is octagonal which, on the interior forms a skeletal framework, allows free circulation of air through it from the basement and out through the louvered cupola. This lessened the danger of spontaneous combustion. The center element is for the storage of hay

Round Barn

which is filled from the second floor of the first element and has a driveway around its entire circumference, allowing the cattle to feed from this perpetual self-leveling hay mow.

On the first floor of the first, or outermost, element are the cattle stanchions and the unique trap doors, located at intervals in the sunken circular trough. These trap doors allow the manure to be shoved down into the basement and piled in heaps under each door.

In the basement of this building a large door admitted a wagon that encircled the basement for the loading of the manure already stacked in heaps under the trap doors.

The diameter of the entire structure is about ninety feet, and the circumference about two-hundred feet. The exterior element is of field stone and the other two elements are of wood.

The initial cost of the Hancock Round Barn was $800. About 1884 the interior of this structure was gutted by fire started by an overturned lantern. All frame material had to be reconstructed.

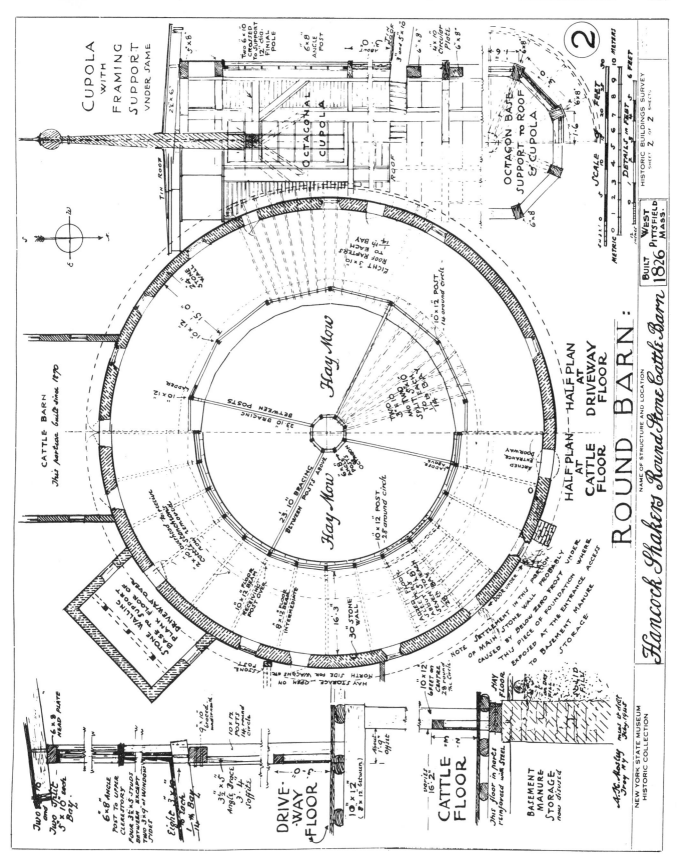

CUPOLA WITH FRAMING SUPPORT UNDER SAME

OCTAGONAL CUPOLA

OCTAGON BASE SUPPORT TO ROOF & CUPOLA

CATTLE BARN This portion built since 1870

Hay Mow

Hay Mow

Hay Mow

HALF PLAN — HALF PLAN AT DRIVEWAY FLOOR AT CATTLE FLOOR

ROUND BARN:

Hancock Shakers Round Stone Cattle Barn

BUILT 1826 WEST PITTSFIELD MASS.

NAME OF STRUCTURE AND LOCATION

SCALE OF FEET

DETAILS IN FEET

HISTORIC BUILDINGS SURVEY SHEET 2 OF 2 SHEETS

NEW YORK STATE MUSEUM HISTORIC COLLECTION

DRIVE-WAY FLOOR

CATTLE FLOOR

BASEMENT MANURE STORAGE now disused

NOTE SETTLEMENT IN THIS PORTION OF MAIN STONE WALL PROBABLY CAUSED BY BELOW ZERO FROST UNDER THIS PIECE OF FOUNDATION WHERE EXPOSED AT THE ENTRANCE ACCESS TO BASEMENT MANURE STORAGE

Inspirational Drawings

A SUGGESTED BIBLIOGRAPHY

EVANS, F. W. (ed.). *Shaker and Shakeress.* Mount Lebanon, N.Y., Vol. 3-4, January 1873-December 1875.

GREEN, CALVIN, and WELLS, SETH Y. *Summary of Views of the Millennial Church,* or *United Society of Believers,* Albany, N.Y., 1848.

MACE, AURELIA. *The Aletheia.* Farmington,. Me., 1899.

MELCHER, MARGUERITE FELLOWS. *The Shaker Adventure.* Princeton, N.J., 1941.

NEAL, JULIA. *By Their Fruits.* University of North Carolina Press, 1947.

NORDHOFF, CHARLES. *The Communistic Societies of the United States.* New York, 1873.

NOYES, JOHN HUMPHREY. *History of American Socialisms.* Philadelphia, Pa., 1870.

ROBINSON, CHARLES EDSON. *Concise History of the Shakers.* East Canterbury, N.H., 1893.

WHITE, ANNA, and TAYLOR, LEILA S. *Shakerism*: *Its Meaning and Message.* Columbus, Ohio, 1905.